*****Simply put, the best book I have ever read!
Dr. Joel Levy (NYC)

Never have I picked up a book at 1 am to read for a few minutes and got so drawn in that I was still reading it when the alarm clock signaled time for work! Holy cow, what a book. From page one, the action never lets up. I ended up finishing the book the next afternoon. It was an incredible roller coaster ride from start to finish. Be warned, if you start this masterpiece, be prepared to finish as you will not be able to put it down. Deserves more than five stars!

*****I truly could not give any other book I've ever read a better review!
Helene M. - Attorney (NYC)

It is very rare for me to read a book in one sitting, but Jerry's wonderful book was able to accomplish what few can. Once you start reading this well-written, thoughtful and honest autobiography, you can not stop. It follows Jerry through most of his life, without relinquishing its thesis from beginning to end. The reader encounters someone who struggles with life on a terrifying level, which we can all relate to on a certain level. It is written for all to enjoy and actually allows us to learn a little about ourselves. The honesty and vivid detail add to the pure enjoyment of reading this book. You will continue to think about this book long after you have finished it. I truly could not give any other book I have ever read a better review.

*****Outstanding entertainment and insight!
Dr. R. Shipon - Author: "Reiki Psychology"

I am deeply grateful to Jerry Castaldo for writing this book. Its pace is so brisk and interesting, with unbelievable scenarios, that it is hard to believe that one man had so many things happen in his life. The way it is presented is incredibly entertaining. This book really MOVES and the reader finds himself befriending Jerry by the end of the book.

Jerry is the ultimate protagonist. If you have ever wondered how good people manage to make the incorrect choices they do, read this book. It holds that kind of wisdom.

This book is down to earth, accessible, fun and interesting. It connects with popular culture and our recent past in a way few other books do. I am deeply moved by Jerry's experiences, his writing, and his generosity in writing such an eye-opening and entertaining personal story.

What a ride! It is a gift to read this book. I feel very lucky for having done so.

*****Breathtakingly fast-paced page turner!
K.R. - Equestrian/Breeder (Wales)

Jerry Castaldo is something like the "Cyborg" in the Terminator movie. He walks through fire, gets up after being smashed to smithereens; skin melting off his frame, head hanging off, and keeps on plodding forward. His honest portrayal of himself is actually almost as scary as it is awe-inspiring. The beauty of the book is that Jerry doesn't know he's a kind of hero. Mostly, he seems to think he's a screw-up, but all the same, he never gives in. Despite himself, he somehow keeps moving toward his goal.

The images he paints of his exploits remain with you for a long time – some even permanently. His struggle and his ultimate emergence into the person he always dreamed of becoming is breathtaking. This book by Jerry Castaldo is a MUST-read!

It is an important body of work for anybody who thinks they can never amount to anything, and for everybody else. I am most certainly richer for having read it!

*******Brave and bold!**
I.G. (Attorney, NYC - Harvard Law Alum)

Jerry spills his guts – literally. It's a smart, compelling, edge-of–your-seat story of an amazing guy. If it weren't so well-written from the heart, you almost wouldn't believe his often harrowing life, the near-misses, etc., but Jerry lets you into his heart and you know it's true. I highly recommend this illuminating, riveting book.

*******From Scuzz...to a BRAND NEW BUZZ!**
C.K. (Radio Show Host, FL)

Honesty makes Jerry Castaldo's memoir a treasure. This is not a ghost written PR piece of fluff that was composed to promote an entertainer to drive ratings. Rather, it's a biography of a life that at one drug induced point its owner deemed not even worth living.

A volatile "cocktail" of intelligence, drive, talent and INCREDIBLE opportunities...combined with hellish alcohol and drug abuse that culminates in waste and disaster.

WARNING! Although this book is a "jewel," it is not necessarily for the skittish, so to speak. "Brooklyn NY: A Grim Retrospective" is exactly what its title suggests, grim! You'll be frustrated, angry and overwhelmed with sadness reading this open, plainly written, extremely brave diary/memoir. This book is NOT a rags to riches piece of fiction. It is a must read for everyone that is living their lives as we all must, one day at a time

*****Powerful and Inspirational!
The Italian Tribune
(America's largest Italian American newspaper)

I wasn't sure at first if I would like this story because I grew up in a totally different atmosphere, although more or less the same era. From the very first page, I was drawn to Jerry's story and kept reading because I felt his emotions jumping out from the pages; making me want to know what happened to him next, what forces shaped his life, and how it would all turn out. Jerry is a real person who writes from the heart and in his struggles and successes he delivers an inspirational message that we can change for the better; sometimes through our own sheer will, and other times with the help of others.

*****Total page turner!!!
Cheryl Stern (NYC) Broadway/Film/TV Actress

You cannot put this book down! I picked it up and read the entire book into the wee hours of the morning. Jerry has taken a long hard ride through crime, drugs, gangs, show biz and a life of addiction and hard knocks and has turned it into fine drama and a truly compelling and uplifting memoir. A natural born story teller, Jerry takes his readers on an extraordinary journey from the depths of hell to a life of sobriety and success with uncanny wit, heart and honesty. This book is a must read!

*****An emotional roller coaster ride!
S.L. (CEO's Office - NJ State)

There was never a dull moment on this emotional roller coaster ride of Jerry Castaldo's life. This is a very brave and valiant effort to share a story that can conceivably help many others who struggle with addiction. Jerry's candor, wit and humor combined with his easy writing style made it simply impossible for me to put the book down; I read it in one sitting. I was sorry to see the book end. Kudos to Jerry for having the guts to tell this story. A book of this caliber is quite a surprise from a first time author.

*****Awards and Applause!
M.M. (Director - Sunrise Corp.)

This is more than a memoir - it is a powerful and brilliant look inside a human soul. Jerry Castaldo's "no holds barred" style of writing takes the reader into his world where you live with him through sometimes horrific, sometimes comical, deeply moving and

v

always compelling chapters of a highly textured life. This is an especially revealing example of humanity at its worst... and at its BEST! An outstanding debut by a truly talented and gifted author - read this book and marvel!

*****Empowering and Well Written!
J.G. - NYC Government

This book is profoundly moving. Page after page evokes different emotions and speaks clearly to the human spirit. An author who wrote a best seller many years ago was told "This is not your book anymore." Well, Jerry Castaldo, I must say, my sentiments exactly. This is not your book anymore, it belongs to the world! Brilliant!

*****A combination of Shakespearean tragicomedy and a modern day Pilgrim's Progress for the new millennium.
Mike Lloyd - United Kingdom

Lurching and careening from one self-made crisis to another, Jerry is besieged by an almost satanic horde of personal demons, a war waged against the innate goodness of his soul. This story is relentless in its power to grip, grasp and engross the reader in Jerry's world.

Brooklyn NY: A Grim Retrospective

Jerry Castaldo

Brooklyn NY: A Grim Retrospective

Brooklyn NY: A Grim Retrospective

Jerry Castaldo

Edited by Chip Deffaa
NY Post Columnist and Author

Jerry Castaldo

THIRD EDITION – APRIL 2012
ISBN: 1450564593
EAN-13: 9781450564595.
Author: Jerry Castaldo
Publisher: Pink Cloud Publishing, NY
Subject: Non-fiction, Autobiography, Addiction, Recovery, Inspiration
Original Publication Date: 8-1-2010
Binding: Paperback
Language: English
Pages: 218   **Dimensions:** 5.5 X 8.5 inches

Printed in the United States of America

"Writing is easy. All you have to do is sit down at a typewriter and bleed."

Ernest Hemingway

Jerry Castaldo

Jerry Castaldo

Jerry Castaldo

Introduction

Why would anyone want to read my story? Who am I? What's the big deal about *my* story? And how could I even write it? I only went to the eighth grade.... Well, maybe six disjointed months of high school, too.

Was I afraid to open up and share all of this? *Yes*.

I've been told time and again over the years that my stories are not just interesting, but are also quite shocking--especially if you know me now. Because of this, many people in my personal life--as well as several in my professional life—have advised me against revealing what I'm about to tell you here.

Am I fearful of being judged and looked upon as a *bad* person? Yes, especially when I've spent the last 19 years rebuilding, retooling, and "re-becoming" the actual person I was as a young boy, before the violence and mayhem. Back when I was an altar boy, a Cub Scout, a Little Leaguer, an uninfluenced child--*innocent.*

What's this book about? It documents my involvement with horrendous crime, rampant drug abuse, gang fighting, jail, in-patient rehabs, psych wards....

Wait! I know exactly what you must be thinking now: *Oh no, not another sappy "I did drugs and was really nuts and then..." story.*

That's only one small element of it. I'd much rather describe it this way.... I so desperately want people to see how a good person is always basically good, regardless of where he or she may falter and go astray; and sometimes--but not always--that person can get back to the beginning. Back to who they were originally, before the "cold cruel world" got a hold on them. Before they were influenced negatively by what they saw and what they experienced around them.

More importantly--in this age of phony, inflated stories that are billed as factual--it's all true. No embellishments. Hard hitting, pushing the limits of human decency--and what is allowed by law to be published without me being prosecuted.

I'm not preaching. And I'm not bragging. I really don't feel special; and I really don't feel all that different from anybody-- that I'm privileged or disadvantaged, that I'm lucky or unlucky.

What I do feel is compelled to speak about this, the following....

Jerry Castaldo

Coney Island Drug Robbery

Summer 1975--Age 16

#1 song on the radio: "Jive Talkin'"—The Bee Gees

With my heart pounding, my breathing quick and shallow--but with surprisingly methodical and efficient strokes--I repeatedly brought the large carpenter's hammer sideways, bashing the face of the Hispanic man clawing at the passenger side window of the car we were fleeing in. The streetlight above was reflecting off some sort of shiny blade he was windmilling at me. I don't remember how many times the blows found their mark; I did see blood.

All evening, this old jalopy of a car that we were riding in was bucking and stalling out. So to think, here at 2 am, with two other Puerto Ricans chasing this ailing car down a dark, deserted street, there was a chance we'd stall. All I can think is: *I should never have gotten in this car with Uncle Tony.*

"Uncle Tony"--as he was known to all in the Bensonhurst, Brooklyn neighborhood that I grew up in-- was older than us; 29 and just paroled from an upstate NY prison. For what, we were never really sure. But he served many years, and we looked up to him for it. You know, the "badge of honor" bullshit.

We all suspected that Uncle Tony was doing heroin. Heroin was a drug that none of us would mess with because that made you a "real" druggie. Barbiturates (downers) like Tuinal and Seconal (which we also called "Gorilla Biscuits" because they made us very violent at

13

times), LSD, pot...all of these were "OK." But doing heroin, whether you snorted it or shot it, made you a real low-life in our eyes. Even so, years later I'd come to find out that many associates of mine did eventually take the plunge into doing the Big H. The common practice of shooting between the toes to hide the track marks was what we concluded Uncle Tony was doing. We still looked up to him, though. After all, he did hard time. He was *crazy*. Being crazy was like being anointed a high priest, like being commissioned a high-ranking officer--a title that traveled with you to other neighborhoods and would get you respect from all. Because then you were feared.

The reason for the car ride with Uncle Tony that hot summer night was not revealed to me beforehand. He just said, "Get in, I gotta do something," and I was more than happy to be taken into his inner circle. I was 16 years old. Had I known that while he left me in an idling, double-parked car, he was going to rob some drug dealers, I probably would never have gotten in. Then again, maybe I would have. I have to admit it: *How could I have not known something bad was going to happen when he said, "Jerry, there's a hammer under the seat."*

"Jerry the Hammer" was the moniker I earned that night. No, I wasn't crazy; no, I didn't want to hit that guy in the face; but yes, I enjoyed the notoriety. Besides, I was afraid of actually being killed that night, so I lashed out like a maniac. It was strictly self-preservation, survival. If I didn't do it, I'd be prey.

The next day at the park where we hung out, it was pleasing to be recognized by the 30 or so other kids that made up the different crews, cliques, gangs, or whatever you want to call them. The older kids acknowledged me; even the girls were wider-eyed than usual with me. This was a good feeling. It meant: *Don't fuck with Jerry Castaldo. He's crazy.*

Beaten to a Bloody Pulp with My Own Hammer

Bay Ridge Section of Brooklyn

A few days later, when I went to the hardware store to buy two large hammers, I never would have imagined they'd both be used on me to bludgeon my head, face, arms, and legs. After all, I was now "Jerry the Hammer."

My mom's boyfriend at the time, John, whom she later married, got me a job loading freight trains in Jersey City, NJ. I lied about my age and said that I was eighteen years old. The guy that hired me didn't even bother to check. It was a grueling, labor-intensive position. Not exactly what I'd want to be doing for the rest of my life. Getting across two rivers to NJ was pretty difficult by train, though--almost a two-hour commute each way. By car I could make it in a half-hour.

After cashing in a life-insurance policy that my grandmother had put in place for me, we found a car for me at the perfect price of $200.00. It was a silver 1965 Dodge Dart sedan and I appreciated it. I bought a small purple steering wheel, installed an eight-track tape player, and fixed it up as best I could. This was great.

Even though most of the kids in the neighborhood had newer cars, this was mine.

I now had a job, a car, and was hoping to distance myself from the "bad" kids that I had been hanging around with. Unfortunately, they wouldn't let me go. In retrospect, I realize I could have broken away somehow; but at the time, I didn't know how to do it.

Sleeping soundly at about twelve one weeknight, I was awakened by yelling outside my bedroom window, which was on the second floor of the apartment building that my brother and I lived in with my mom and her boyfriend. "Castaldo, hey Castaldo," I heard. It was them. The thieves, the liars, the so-called "friends" who I now realize were nothing more than fellow gang members. I tried to ignore them, but then they started throwing stuff at my window. "Okay, okay, I'll be right down," I said.

Junior was the leader of our own crew of six guys-- which is kind of funny, because he was the short, small one. But he was *crazy* and had proved it numerous times around the neighborhood. Now at 16 years of age, he had already been arrested many times, and had been in and out of Spofford Correctional Facility for Youths in the Bronx.

"We need to go 'bageling'," Junior said-- which was another term for popping trunks to steal the radial tires, which reminded us of giant bagels. Each tire was worth $25.00 to the neighborhood fence. Using a large screwdriver sharpened to a point, Philly, the biggest, strongest one of us, would push a hole into the trunk, right next to the keyhole of a late-model luxury car.

Then, a lit match was dropped into the hole so you could see where to insert a regular flathead screwdriver sideways to "pop" the lock open. Even when there was an alarm, we would lift the trunk lid, quickly unscrew the mount that held the tire and then take off before the windows on all of the houses started lighting up. There'd be times when people—still in their underwear--were coming toward us waving bats, and we'd barely make it out of there.

"I can't do that, I've got a job now. I gotta get up at 5:30 in the morning," I hollered back. I was then told that if I wasn't coming out, I'd better hand over my keys and let them use the car. The rest of the goons hovered nearby waiting for my reply. After several no's, I finally gave in and relinquished the keys. I told them to make sure they bent the license plates up so they couldn't be read. *This was so fucked-up; my new car now was being used to commit crimes while I slept.* I begged them to bring back the car and leave the keys in the ashtray when they were done.

The next morning, the car was there in its usual spot and I went to work. They told me that they had stopped at three stolen tires because they couldn't fit any more in the car. So, they didn't want this small vehicle of mine anymore. Thank God! Let them use stolen Lincoln Continentals like they usually did. Lots of room in the trunk.

Out of everyone in the neighborhood, Stevie Bones was my best friend. A while back, when he was 14 years old, people started calling him "Bones" because of how skinny he was. He hated it, but it stuck. We were the "good" kids who went to grammar school together. Then we started hanging out with "them." We both had slowly morphed into unimportant little street thugs after getting involved with Junior and the others. It made us both change for the worse from then on. What happened was that even when the two of us were alone and not in the company of the crew, we started doing things on our own that were bad. Very bad. It was like a communicable virus had infected us. *Fuck life; it all sucks. Take what you want-- steal, fight; get all you can get now. The world blows. If we die, we die.*

Many around us did indeed die.

One Saturday night while Stevie Bones and I were cruising in my car on 86th street, a popular thoroughfare--with Barry White's Love Unlimited Orchestra blaring from the speakers--we ventured out of Bensonhurst and headed into the next neighboring area called Bay Ridge.

"What the fuck are you looking at?" Stevie yelled at the carload of guys that was stopped next to us at a red light. This pipsqueak friend of mine, Stevie, who I don't ever remember winning a fist fight, was suddenly a tough guy with a big mouth. All it took was some Tuinals and hundred proof Southern Comfort. The guys in the car started yelling back. The light turned green and we drove on. In the rear-view mirror, I could see them all waving their fists at us. They pulled up beside us again and we yelled some more; and they yelled back, both of our cars bucking and jockeying for position.

"Muthafuckas! Stevie, the hammer is under your seat," I said. This was sort of the same line Uncle Tony had given me. After buying the hammers, I had placed my newly acquired weapons under the two front seats; now it looked like they were going to be put into action.

After turning left and right down several streets, I could see again in my rear-view mirror that they were still following us. We came to a stop sign on a deserted, middle-class, residential street. They pulled around and out in front of us and stopped their car, blocking us. Quickly, they all scrambled out. *Holy shit--five guys against two!*

Before we could get out, they had pulled our doors open. Now two of them were trying to pull me out. While still swinging my hammer with one hand, I tried to hold onto the steering wheel with the other, to avoid being dragged out. It felt futile. The others were trying to drag Stevie out, too. Somehow I got the car into reverse and hit the gas. We sped violently backward, tires screeching, the open driver's-side door dragging one of the guys back with us. As we zig-zagged in reverse, the edge of the open door started hitting the parked cars lining the street--and this guy was still in between the crashing door and the parked cars. I remember thinking: *He looks like he's dancing a ballet, or being electrocuted in slow motion.* Finally he disappeared under the door, and at that moment the front left tire bumped up and over something. *Was that him?*

Thinking I had just crushed and killed him, I continued racing in reverse all the way down the block. We went right through the two-lane intersection, still going backwards; we were lucky that no cars were coming in either direction. I made it about another 100 feet into the next block before I lost control. The trunk of my car smashed into the front of a parked car. The tremendous impact made both Stevie and me hit back against the front seat so hard that it was knocked down flat.

"Look!" Stevie said as we both tried to comprehend what had just happened. I squinted through the windshield and saw all of them running toward us. I told Stevie to get out and fight, but before we could do anything, they were upon us. This time they did manage to pull me out. I swung my hammer--missing, not connecting. While swinging wildly, at one point I actually hit myself. *What the fuck!?! I thought I was a tough guy. But now I'm getting my friggin' assed kicked in!*

After they had gotten me on the ground and were kicking me, they realized that they could not get the hammer from my hands. I just wouldn't let go. I kept thinking: *"If they take this, they'll use it on me."* My eyes were closed now--a big mistake. There was no escape. It was then that I realized I was being hit in the legs with another hammer--Stevie's hammer! They'd taken his from him, and roughed him up a little bit, before he ran down the street and got away. Now they wanted me.

I distinctly remember the first blow that I received to my temple. It reminded me of those cartoons—you know, where you hear a "boing" when one of the characters hits another on the head, and then they hear "tweet tweet"--like birds or something. Amidst all of this punching and kicking, and yelling and screaming that they were doing—"You ran over my friend, you motherfucker!"--I was thinking of cartoons. Bam! A second shot to my head! At this point I didn't feel any

20

pain at all; I just relaxed my head on the cool black pavement of the street and decided to stop fighting. Bam! A third shot!

"OK, OK, that's enough," the other guy yelled, "--you're gonna kill him!"

I'm not sure if I was playing dead because I was afraid and wanted them to stop, or because it just felt so good to relax and lay there--but whatever the reason I did what I did, it worked. I think they ran because they thought that I was dead or dying. As I lay there, relieved that it was finally over, I could hear the sound of crashing glass—they were smashing every window on my car, along with the headlights. I then heard their car doors slam shut, and the sound of them driving away. What a beautiful silence I was experiencing! I could feel a lot of warm blood streaming down my face. I just stayed right there, not moving, fading in and out of consciousness.

When I eventually staggered to my feet, I saw that Stevie was stumbling toward me, back to the scene, out of hiding. They had beaten him only with their hands and feet because his hammer was used to get me to release my hammer. He had blood on his head and a little on his arm. People were now coming out of their houses, in their robes and slippers, and telling us that the cops were on their way. But I wouldn't accept help. I just wanted to get out of there.

"Stevie, come on; get in the car," I told him. He was bleeding, I was bleeding. The car's back looked like an accordion; the left front door was bent open and wouldn't shut; the front seat was broken and down flat. We had no lights any more; the windows were all shattered. For a moment, I thought we should drive ourselves to Victory Memorial Hospital for treatment. *But wait--No, I can't! What if that bump I felt back then was me running over that guy? What if he dies? Where is he? Did his friends take him to a hospital?*

I decided instead to first report the car stolen and abandon it. Then we could go to the hospital for help. I thought that I was so smart. *Yeah, if I say someone stole the car, I couldn't be held responsible for crashing into that parked car or possibly killing anybody.* So we drove to a quiet "Lover's Lane" type of area called Shore Parkway. (It was actually the exact spot where, two summers later-- July 31st, 1977—"Son-of-Sam Killer" David Berkowitz would murder his last victim, Stacy Moskowitz.) I parked the car.

"What the fuck are you doing?" moaned Stevie. He couldn't believe what he was seeing. There was no way I was going to leave my new eight-track stereo in it! What a scene; it was almost comical. My face is all bloody and swelling like a football--and I'm looking for my tools so I can remove the stereo!

We lied to the emergency room staff at the hospital and scribbled phony contact information down on the forms that they handed us. After hours of waiting, we were sewn up and released. Stevie and I dragged ourselves to the bus stop as the early morning sun slowly rose. After being out all night, it was time to go home.

As I think back to those times, I realize that I was truly uncontrollable; my mother was probably at her wit's end, dealing with me. Walking into our apartment that morning, I'm sure I scared the shit out of her--and the neighbors, too. My mother opened the door and there I was--limping, steadying myself with a cane, and with the most grotesque-looking face, stitches crossing my forehead. You know those fright films where the actress lets out those blood-curdling shrieks? That was my mom: "Oh my God, what happened, what happened, what happened?"

That evening, I endured a slow, carefully maneuvered shower. Afterwards, it was an excruciatingly painful experience just to dress myself. I then grabbed my cane and limped five city blocks over to the park. And I looked like shit. *That's right; I was going to hang out at the park now.* I just couldn't let this great opportunity pass. *Everybody will see me like this. Another valiant battle fought. Score!* Once again, validation.

A wide-eyed, salivating crowd circled me and stood in awe as I told the story through a deformed, swollen mouth. The cane and limping added extra drama. Many of the guys patted me on the back, shook my hand, looked at each other and laughed, saying, "Shit, man-- Jerry Castaldo is fuckin' crazy."

Perfect, just what I wanted to hear--another notch in my belt. I'm safe here in this environment. People are afraid of me; good!

There was never anything made of my reporting my car stolen; there were no repercussions from what happened that night. Who knows what happened to that guy? I never saw my car again. And I didn't want to own a hammer anymore.

don't buy a
hammer)!!

Stab Me, Jerry—Harder!

Fall 1975--Age 16

#1 song on the radio: "That's The Way I Like It"—KC and the Sunshine Band

"Jerry, get up. Jerry, your friend is here; get up." Mustering the strength to roll my body over, and separate my crusted-over eyelids, I could see the blurry vision of my mother standing in the doorway of the bedroom that my younger brother Ken and I shared. Of course, I was hung over from the usual, always potentially fatal--or at least potentially brain-damaging-- cocktail of pills and alcohol from the night before. I didn't even remember the night before. Amnesia was a regular thing for me.

It was a Saturday morning at about ten and the friend-- now replacing my mom and standing next to my bed, in my degraded field of vision--was Johnny. Known in the neighborhood of Bath Beach as Johnny Reb—the term "Reb" being short for "rebel"--he was three years older than me and well-liked by everyone. Personally, I didn't know why he was such a "rebel." He never really demonstrated--at least, not to me anyway--anything that would designate him as such; no fights, no serious crimes. To me, he was just a really nice guy with a barely noticeable stutter. It was such a relief to see that it was Johnny in my room and not the detective from the local police precinct who recently had been stopping by and trying to catch me at home to "talk." Since he never found anyone at home, he'd always leave his card taped to the door and I'd make sure to take it away before my mother would find it. I guess he did this because we didn't have a telephone for him to call us on. He eventually gave up.

Bay 22nd Street, between Bath Avenue and Cropsey Avenue in Brooklyn, was where Johnny Reb's crew hung out. There was a TV series in the '70s called "Welcome Back Kotter," starring John Travolta as Vinny Barbarino. If you watch the first few scenes of the introduction that is shown while a wimpy-sounding guy sings the title song, "Welcome Back," you can see the exact group of dilapidated apartment buildings that we would congregate in and around.

I'm not really sure why or how this happened to be, but I was different from most of the other kids who belonged to the various cliques that were around back then. Most of the others would hang out only with their own crew, which was usually close to home, in the area where they lived. But I would travel to different neighborhoods and find a way to "get in" with different groups. Bay 22nd Street was a half-hour city bus-ride away for me, but whether I was hanging out in my local park, or in any of the about five different sections of Brooklyn that I frequented, my rep was always intact. I experienced minor local-celebrity status in all of those locations. For even if you didn't admire me, chances are you were a just a little bit afraid of me; the insane, violent stories were out there.

Back then—and still, to this day--I considered myself a chameleon. Later in life, I have found this to be a valuable commodity, especially in business. There were some guys in the other crews who also yearned to be known as "crazy"; they were the only ones who would put me down. It was always a competition. They'd always try to find some way to downplay or slightly skew the stories being told about me to pump themselves up.

"Johnny, what the fuck you doin' here? I'm sleepin', man," I told him.

He started, "Yo, Jerry, I really need your help. You know that girl from the block that I'm seeing? Well, I have to work today. I really want to take off so I can stay with her, but I'm afraid they'll fire me."

"They" being the local supermarket--formerly an A&P, and now owned and run by the Aiello family. Antoinette Aiello--who was a man despite the female-sounding name--was the owner. I was a stock boy there for a short while who prided himself on having every label in my tuna-fish aisle perfectly aligned. Johnny was in the produce section. The owner had a nephew, Ron Aiello, who worked there, too. He was about 15 years older than us. The actor Danny Aiello was reportedly a cousin, so Ron was able to weasel his way into small acting roles here and there. Years later I saw him playing a barber in director Sidney Lumet's 1981 film "Prince of The City" with Treat Williams.

"So whatta ya want from me?" I asked. I slowly sat up into a sitting position with my blanket still covering my lower body. "Just call in sick," I told him.

"Nah," Johnny said. "Fuckin' Irving says that if I call in sick again, or am late again, I'm gone."

Irving was the store manager, which we found kinda odd, because he was a Jewish guy in his late fifties who didn't quite blend in with the general Italian atmosphere of the store, the customers; the neighborhood.

"I was thinkin'," Johnny said. "If you could stab me, maybe in my leg, then I can take off a few days and not get fired."

After a bit of a pause--as I sat there, still half asleep--I processed what Johnny Reb was asking me to do, and then broke into loud laughter. "Ha, ha, you crazy fuck. Whatta you gotta do that for? Just call in sick, man!"

I'm not sure why I always laughed at horrific-sounding things, but it obviously started at a young age. Even now, I sometimes laugh when I'm presented with a scary or disturbing story. Maybe it's some sort of an emotional defense mechanism. I do know that as an adult, it can be politically incorrect to exhibit this, and so--depending on the company I'm with—I sometimes must mask this weird reaction that I have.

After a few minutes of trying to talk him out of it--and with him begging me to do it--I gave in. We decided that we'd go to the local playground and I'd stab him there. I opened the bottom drawer of my dresser and reached all the way to the back, where--hidden under some old clothes that I never wore, where my unsuspecting mother would never look—I kept my 007 knife. I got the knife, got dressed, and we left.

On the way to the playground, I suggested that we should buy a quart of Budweiser Beer for him to slug down beforehand. I quickly added that we should buy two quarts--one for me, as well. We pooled the change in our pockets and made sure we had cigarettes, too. We walked, we drank, we smoked. And we decided that the side of his thigh, right below the buttocks, would be the best spot for the stabbing. We tried to psyche each other out.

Johnny, picking up his pace excitedly, was breathing hard now. He was sucking down smoke, and blowing it out, yelling, "Come on muthafucka, let's do this!"

I, on the other hand, was a bit worried. *Should I push it straight in or on an angle, shallow or deep, quickly or slowly?* I mentioned that we should get a rag, a tee-shirt, or something like that in case we have to tie off any unexpected surge of blood. We both thought that this was a good idea, so we stopped back at my apartment building to get something.

Mothers with their kids were playing in different areas of the park when we got there. I told Johnny that we probably should choose the monkey bars so he could hold onto them while I stab him. We had to wait a few minutes until the few kids in the monkey-bar area moved away. The parents actually started ushering them away sooner than we had thought they would. I guess Johnny and I were conspicuous—repeatedly looking over in their direction, while drinking large beers out of brown paper bags. It was only 11 in the morning.

Walking onto the soft black padding surrounding the monkey bars, which was put down by the NYC Parks Department to dampen any falls by children, we looked around suspiciously. We had some privacy, but not a lot. It was a sunny day and the playground was starting to fill up. "Take both hands and hold onto the bars right about here, shoulder height," I instructed him. I looked around, took my 007 knife out of my back pocket, and unfolded it. This was the biggest folding pocket-knife you could get. I had once been caught by my teacher selling these knives in grammar school. The blade alone was six inches long, so when the knife was opened up, the entire length of the handle and blade came to about a foot. I remember wishing I had a smaller knife.

Johnny held the bars tightly, closed his eyes, and shouted, "Come on, do it, do it!" My grip on the handle of the knife was so tight, I was worried that the blade would penetrate too deeply into his thigh. So I loosened my grip a little, looked around, and then half-heartedly pushed the shiny silver tip of the blade into his jeans.

"Ah, ah, ah, fuck, shit, ah--" Johnny cried out. He was hopping around like a pogo stick, grimacing with pain.

I started yelling, "I'm sorry, I'm sorry; Johnny, I'm sorry." I looked around nervously. "Let me see, let me see; stop moving, so I can see," I told him. Looking down, I could only see a very faint, almost non-existent, tiny blotch of blood on his jeans. The knife had barely broken the surface of his skin.

"You didn't push it in hard enough, Jerry," Johnny moaned. I told him again that I was sorry, and promised to try again.

The few parents and kids that were still in the park were now far away. I'm sure they could see that something weird was going on. "All right, hold on, I'm gonna do it," I warned Johnny. This time I gripped the knife tighter, hoping that now I could get it in further, even though I didn't want the entire blade to go in. I brought my arm back behind me to get a little momentum, and then brought the blade forward into his thigh in the same area.

"Ow, ow, ow, ow!" Johnny called out. He started hopping around again, in pain. And I'm yelling, "I'm sorry, sorry, sorry." We looked to see how much blood there was. To our horror, there was not much more than before.

"What the fuck are you doin', Jerry? You still didn't get it in good enough." I explained that I was afraid of pushing too hard and sending it to too far in. He was in pain, but we were failing; he was not injured "enough." I then had a brainstorm.

"How about I punch you right in the face and blacken your eye? You can say you got jumped," I blurted out.

Johnny said, "OK, good idea, let's try that."

I added, "We should go to the grocery store and get a roll of quarters. I'll put them inside of my fist before I punch you. I'll be able to really fuck your face up good."

We left the playground with Johnny slightly limping, his face all scrunched up from the pain and his right leg bleeding just a bit. The red bloodstain on his blue pants leg was only about two inches in diameter. I was trying to figure out who we could ask to lend us the money so we could buy the roll of quarters when Johnny pulled out a twenty-dollar bill. I shouted, "Fuckin' hold-out, you are!" Here we were scrounging for pocket-change for the beer, and he had a twenty on him all the time.

Back at the playground about a half-hour later, I had Johnny brace himself, holding onto a sprinkler pipe. I placed the roll of quarters in my right hand. How strange his face looked! It was a different expression from when I was stabbing him. He had his head tilted back a little, with his chin protruding forward, sort of exaggerated. His eyes were tightly closed. He looked like a peculiar statue. I told him to get ready. I wound up and—aiming carefully so as not to miss and break his nose--I punched him right in the eye. Breaking loose his grip from the pipe, he started jumping around on his one good leg yelling, "Shit, oh shit, shit, shit!"

I started yelling, "I'm sorry, sorry; I'm sorry Johnny." We walked over to the curb of the sidewalk, right outside of the playground, and turned a car's side-view mirror around so that he could see how his eye looked.

"You didn't punch me hard enough, fucker," Johnny complained. There was a very slight red mark around his eye orbit, but not much more.

"OK, OK, let's try again," I offered.

At this point, I just wanted to get the whole thing over with. I decided that I was going to hit him with everything I've got. He grabbed onto the pipe again, I gripped the roll of quarters tightly in my fist, wound up again, wider than before, and punched him in the face as if my life depended on it.

Not only did Johnny stagger around, moaning in pain, but I too danced an awkward Irish Jig --the roll of quarters had crushed my fingers! They started swelling up like little balloons. But, more importantly, by the next morning Johnny had raccoon eyes. He spent the next few days with his girlfriend--off from work with no retribution.

Grand Theft Auto

Spring 1976--Age 17

#1 song on the radio: "Oh, What a Night—The Four Seasons"

Driving a car was for me--as I'm sure it is for many teenagers--a thrilling adventure, a realization of freedom, independence. You could just roll along the streets and venture out to other neighborhoods-- even Manhattan. You were almost an adult now. You were in control of something "big." I just loved to drive, probably more than anything else at that time; it was such an escape. I just had to figure out how to get enough money so that I could buy another used car.

Since my dad had left some years back, my mom was always working and struggling to raise my brother and I. My father had taken up with a blonde, "exotic" dancer who was twenty-five years younger than him and who danced under the stage name "Bobbie Lane." She would do this bizarre routine with her huge, bare breasts that involved lit candles or something. I never actually saw her act, but I do know that my brother did, courtesy of a wholesome, weekend outing with my father. I missed not seeing my dad much, although some of the extreme violence that he'd exhibited had frightened me when I was a young child. I remember once, after he had assaulted a cop, breaking the cop's nose, he was beaten by several policemen with clubs and sustained over one-hundred stitches to his head. Another time, later on when I was older, a local mob guy and his cronies were gunning for my father over some business dispute and he had to avoid going to certain places. They finally caught up with my dad one night near the waterfront, shooting out the streetlight to make it dark while they tried to pull him into their car. Luckily, he fought them off somehow and was able to get away. They never were able to get at him again though, because a month later that mobster was himself gunned down and killed in a Manhattan nightclub called *Bedrock*, a club that I would go to once in a while.

So, my dad was there on the periphery, fading in and out of our lives, giving "some" cash to my mom (who had a big heart, and never wanted to force him into court for structured child-support payments to us). It seems to me that it was somewhere back in the mid-'70s when dual-income families started becoming more common, where both parents would be out in the work-force all day. So, it was no big deal to me, as I remember it, that my mother was working. I was a "latch-key kid," coming home from school to an empty apartment with no real supervision until 6 pm or so.

In addition, a few years earlier, when I was about twelve years old, my mother had been physically disabled in a horrific car accident. (The local newspaper plastered a photo of her—bloody and unconscious, being pulled from a crumpled-up car—on the front page.). This accident prevented her from working for a couple of years.

What I'm trying to say is that by now there was very little money. We didn't even have a phone in our apartment, and we had to endure the embarrassing task of handing over food stamps to grocery clerks-- sometimes when my friends were around to see. Once in a while we'd try to buy non-food items with those stamps, but then the annoyed cashier would stop the whole line and loudly, clearly tell us that we had to put those items back.

Then there were also the occasional eight-hour marathon waiting-sessions, every once in a while-- just standing in line at the Welfare office in downtown Brooklyn to qualify for benefits. I'll never forget how, one cold, dark and windy winter morning, my mom woke my brother and me up at six o'clock so we could get down there and be one of the first families on line. Just getting up was such a struggle because it seemed that we never had enough heat or hot water, so my mother would fire up the gas jets on the kitchen stove to help warm up this tiny eight-foot-by-five-foot room we called a kitchen. It's kind of funny for me to think back to those days, because now I realize that we were burning all of the breathable oxygen out of the air with this lame heating method, leaving only carbon dioxide to inhale. I think we were kind of lucky to skirt the headline, "Mother and Two Children Dead of Asphyxiation."

When we got down to the Welfare office, at about seven on this one particular morning, we couldn't believe it--there were already dozens of other people standing like cattle, on a long line in the freezing winter cold, outside of the locked office doors. After the doors were opened at eight o'clock, several City workers started barking orders to us to start filing in. As the line moved into the outer hallway and stopped again, many people-- already exhausted from standing for hours outside--sat down on the filthy staircase and even on the floor. I remember looking over at this very large woman with one of those big beehive hair styles that women used to wear back in the '60s. For some reason, my gaze just sort of lingered on her head--I guess because there was nothing else around to look at, except the wall. All of a sudden I saw this giant cockroach crawl right out of her hair and onto the wall behind her! I looked at my mom, pointed to what I was seeing, and I remember her putting her hand over her mouth, grimacing, and making the "I wanna vomit right now" face. My brother Ken just laughed.

I don't think it was this particular day, but on another similar day, that we waited from early morning to late in the afternoon to see a caseworker. My poor mother was devastated when, after all these hours of waiting, we were told by this caseworker--with not an ounce of sympathy—"Oh no, you don't have the correct documentation; you have to come back tomorrow." After my mother inquired if we could then avoid the whole "waiting in line" thing because we had only forgotten some paperwork, she sternly replied, "No, you have to wait in line just like everybody else," then yelled out, "Next!," and coldly turned away from us.

As an adult, I now realize that—besides the fact that these city workers may not have been the "cream of the crop" of administrative personnel-- this type of unforgiving behavior may have been promoted by management to discourage anyone who was just plain lazy, and didn't want to work, from getting Welfare benefits. As a child, though, it simply hurt me very much, and made me very sad, to see these "mean" adults treat us--and all of the other people who were in the same boat--so badly.

Jerry Castaldo

Eventually, my mother recovered, partially, from her severe injuries stemming from the car accident, and she was able to work again at a modest-paying job. Between her and her live-in boyfriend, ten years her junior, contributing with his also-modest income, things were slightly better again. But we were still pretty broke.

A 1965 Pontiac Bonneville that polluted the air with blue smoke, had a noisy muffler, and a variety of other mechanical ailments, was the family car. I had accidentally discovered that the ignition assembly was broken, and found that I could start the car without the key by inserting a bent wire coat-hanger into the ignition. I'd just drive the car away without my mom knowing it. Many nights I would do this, while also making sure to put garbage cans in the parking spot. This was so I could put the car back in the exact same spot and she wouldn't know that I was taking it every night--usually after midnight when I'd sneak out. I started doing this at about age 15--no license, no insurance card or registration, no driving experience. I'd sometimes drive around solo and sometimes pick up some of my cronies, but I always had an adventure.

As my passion for driving grew, I needed to drive more, all the time--during the daytime hours, too. I couldn't wait for the middle of the night anymore. Somehow, I was always able to find a job here and there as a teenager-- but nothing that could support my buying another car at this particular time.

When I hear the words "car thief," I think of a bad person, someone who is an uncaring part of society. Someone who should earn their own money to buy their own things and toe the line with the "good" people and behave. A car thief steals from people who work hard for their money; he or she should be put in jail. I assumed at that time, as I still do, that most younger car thieves are in that business to make money by bringing their ill-gotten gains to places like "chop shops," that in turn dissect vehicles for illegal sale of individual parts to unsavory business owners.

I'm prefacing the upcoming story with all of this background, for one reason. I never did have--nor do I have as an adult,--larceny in my heart. I was then--and consider myself now--a hard worker who doesn't expect a free ride in life. At that time, I was psychologically (as well as, at various times, physically) addicted to hard drugs. Suicide was a common thought. At many different times during my teenage years, I just didn't care about life. I felt I was given a bad break, that my family was given a bad break, that nothing mattered--that the entire world was so screwed up, that I could do anything I wanted and feel justified because I was in such pain. To be honest with you, if someone told me this same story-- even if they told me that they only did this stuff as a teenager and would never do it now as an adult-- I'd still be afraid to trust them. I guess its human nature. But the absolute truth of the matter is that, in my pre-teen years, I was an honest person, and today I am once again one of the most honest and trustworthy persons you're liable to find. When I didn't care about living and didn't care if I died, however, I would forsake everything and everybody. Yes, this former altar boy had fallen to the lowest depths of despair.

So, I drove. How? *Stolen cars.* All types, all makes, all models, all years. Was this for financial gain? Nah, I just wanted to drive--have the radio blaring, and drive anywhere, everywhere.

No, I never learned to "hot-wire" a car. That called for choosing the correct wires from under the dashboard and then splicing them together in some "magical" configuration. I needed a car with the keys in it that I could then own for a few days; the "bending the coat hanger trick" that I so successfully employed to start my mom's car wouldn't work.

My solution: There was a neighborhood food establishment that had such a thriving business, that on any given Friday or Saturday evening, there would be four, five, six or seven cars double-parked outside of it, starting from about eight o'clock and continuing until about midnight. The owners of these vehicles all made the same mistake, over and over again-- almost all of them left their motors running with the keys in the ignition.

I often would arrive within the "window of opportunity," jump in--and just drive off. I did this so many times that eventually the owners of the establishment put up a sign on the wall saying, "Please do not leave keys in car." People ignored that sign. Many more cars disappeared.

After a day or two, I'd realize that the car was now on the so-called "hot sheet" and I'd have to relinquish my temporary ownership. Believe it or not, once in a while-- if the registration was in the glove compartment--I'd actually call the person from a public phone and tell them where the car was parked so they could get it back. I'd say that the keys were in the ashtray and that I was sorry. I figured that this would help me in the long run somehow, by both relieving my guilt and halting any further investigation by the cops regarding this offense known simply as grand theft, auto.

One Saturday night I was hunched over, tip-toeing toward the driver side of a targeted running car, just about to grab the handle to open the car door, when I heard, "Jerry, what are you doing?" It was my mother! She and her boyfriend John were driving by and pulled over to see what I was doing.

I stopped, turned around and sort of laughed it off and stammered, "Nothing, I'll be home later," and quickly walked away and around the corner. As I've said before, I was uncontrollable.

There was another time when this straight-laced older kid, Larry, had embarrassed me in front of some girls. His family had money, he had a brand new car, and he would always find a way to put me down in front of others. I decided that I'd go to his house and talk to him. It was drizzling that day. I stood on the front stoop and rang the bell. His dad answered. I nervously asked him to call his son out to talk.

After a minute or so, Larry came out. He didn't have a shirt on, and was puffing up his chest. (A weightlifter, he was showing off.) And he was chomping on an apple. He had this smirk on his face that seemed to say, *"What do YOU want and why are you here at MY house?"* I tried to nicely tell him that I was upset with the way he'd poke fun at me in front of other kids. He just kept smirking with this stupid, goofy look on his face, and biting off these big "man-size" chunks of the apple, seeming not to care about how serious I was about this. After repeated futile attempts to garner any empathetic feedback from him, I decided my efforts were to no avail.

I wound up and punched him square in the face!

We wound up grappling, falling off the side of the stoop and into the front flower bed. The dirt was muddy from the rain. The mud eventually covered us both from head to toe, as I punched, kicked, clawed and finally bit into his left pectoral muscle--leaving, I later found out, a row of my teeth-marks in his chest.

Larry's dad came out. I guess he was trying to break us up. But as he held onto me, it just allowed his son to get a few extra punches into my face. When I was finally free, I just got up and ran.

The acquisition of my next stolen car was not really for joyriding. I now had to secure a "tool"--a tool I could use to exact payback on Larry.

"Rosalie, come on out; it's Jerry," I yelled. Rosalie was a local girl, a year or so older than me, who I'd hang out with once in a while. I was honking the horn outside of the apartment she shared with her Italian-immigrant mother who spoke almost no English. The window blinds shook for a moment. I could see someone separate them enough to look out and see who was honking. Then Rosalie raised the blinds. I hollered, "Come out!" She told me to wait a few minutes.

As we drove around, she commented on what a nice car I had and I said "Thanks," without elaborating. Little did she know that I intended this to be my "weapon" that I'd use to take vengeance on the "apple chomper." It was still too early for me to execute my plan, so I suggested that we go to the liquor store.

Several hours later, at about 11:30 pm, I was ready. Unfortunately, Rosalie seemed to have had too much to drink. She was now acting "loopy" and saying that she felt sick to her stomach. I got her something to eat. I then turned the car around and headed for Larry's house.

Larry had this beautiful new Pontiac Grand Prix. It was parked along the curb, by his family's tidy little brick home. I pulled "my" car up so that it was perpendicular to his car, with the back of my car facing the driver's side of his car. I told Rosalie to lie down in the front seat because I didn't want her to get whiplash.

I pulled my car away from his, a bit, to make sure I could gain the necessary momentum. Then I stopped, looked around, put my car into reverse, and then floored the accelerator pedal. We screeched in reverse for a couple of seconds before violently ramming into Larry's new car. I hit that Grand Prix hard enough so that I actually pushed it sideways and up onto the curb. His alarm went off, producing a deafening wail that filled the air of this nicely-kept block of homes.

Rosalie quickly sat up, opened her eyes, and started screaming "What's happening, Jerry, what's happening?" I screeched away. She started puking.

Larry and I eventually lost touch with each other. We didn't talk for many years, and I never expected to see him again. Then something quite ironic occurred. After falling down a flight of subway stairs in the early '80s while inebriated, I was taken to an emergency room with severe cuts to my forehead and lower lip.

To my surprise, Larry was now a physician specializing in plastic surgery. We spoke briefly, never mentioning the problems of the past; it was as if we were just two old friends—the best of friends. His benevolence moved me to tears. Although I didn't have any medical coverage except for what the Army had given me when I was discharged in 1980 --the Veterans Administration doesn't cover cosmetic surgery--he saw how badly I would be scarred, and offered, free of charge, to do the needed work.

He never knew it was me who demolished his car; for if he did, he could have taken that opportunity and could have really "rearranged" my face.

The Mob, the Bookie and the Leisure Suits

Fall 1976--Age 17

#1 song on the radio: "Disco Duck"—Rick Dees

It really never occurred to me that I could someday steal the "wrong" person's car. You know-- a person who, if they were ever to catch you, would take the law into their own hands and not want to involve the police. Someone who could make you "disappear."

The roof of the four-story apartment building that I lived in had a black tar surface, which was commonly referred to--as were most similar roofs in Brooklyn—as tar beach. All you needed was a folding lounge-chair, a radio, a beer and a joint, a shiny silver "melanoma producing" sun reflector to focus the sun's damaging rays on your face, a concoction of baby oil mixed with iodine-- and you were "at the beach."

I was thoroughly enjoying such a day when I suddenly heard a gruff voice coming from one of two, large imposing figures standing over me and blocking my sun. "Ehh... You're Jerry Castaldo, right?" asked the bigger guy, who seemed to be in his late forties.

"Yeah, yeah, that's him," said the other one. As I squinted into the sunlight, holding my hand in a "saluting" position over my eyes, I recognized this one; his name was Nunzio, he was in his mid-thirties, and he lived in my building.

"Yo, Fuck--Howdya' like we throw you off the roof?" said the older one.

45

Nunzio tried to calm him down: "Easy, easy, I know this kid."

I was pretty relieved because even though I had no clue as to what I had done, I was immediately conjuring up images of being thrown to my death from this roof.

"What did I do, what did I do?" I asked. "Nunzio, you know me. I didn't do nothing! Who is this guy?"

Nunzio explained that someone had stolen his boss's car, and they heard it was me. The other guy then said, "Come on, get dressed; you're coming with us. You gotta talk to the Boss." I quickly started scanning my memory, trying to figure out which car it must have been--the Lincoln Continental, the Caddy....

"Alright, alright," I replied. "Just let me get my clothes out of my apartment and I'll come down to the front of the building." The big guy then advised me that I shouldn't fuck around; I should hurry up.

As we were driving, I tried asking them where we were going to; I was told to shut up. It seemed like Nunzio wasn't the important one in this duo, just a flunky. The drive ended sooner than I expected--just five minutes away from where I lived, at The Mayflower Moving and Storage Warehouse. I started having images of me being chopped up into little pieces and then transported away in a moving truck to some final burial ground they had picked out for me.

"Get the fuck in there!" the big guy ordered, as he motioned me toward the front door of the warehouse. I was led into a large open area with nothing around except for one chair. He told me, "Sit in the fuckin' chair scumbag! The Boss will be here soon." I sat down; my right leg started twitching involuntarily.

I hadn't a clue who this "boss" guy was, who was coming to talk to me. I hadn't known that my neighbor Nunzio was associated with anyone like this. Nunzio had a wife and two daughters, and kept to himself. As I sat there thinking about it, though, it did seem like he didn't work regular hours; he came and went at weird times.

Suddenly a big, tall guy who looked like a movie gangster right out of central casting walked in and asked, "Nunzio--this the fuck that stole the Boss's car?" Nunzio told him yes. The guy then walked over to me, towering over my chair. He laughed maniacally and hissed, "Oh man, are you fucked." Now both of my legs were twitching.

It must have taken a half-hour or more for "the Boss" to get there. All the while I'm trying to plan my strategy. *Do I cry and try to get sympathy? Or do I act tough and maybe I'll get a job with them?* I really didn't know with whom they were associated. Bensonhurst was--and still is--Mafia land, although no one uses that word much. The Gambino family seemed to be the dominant faction from what I could infer from reading the papers at that time. The leader of the family, Carlo Gambino had just died in October of a heart attack at age 74. The reason I remember this is because he had succeeded the callous Albert Anastasio, a gangster who I'll tell you more about later.

Jerry Castaldo

Right across the street from this warehouse was a cocktail lounge named "Tali's." Although we were under-age, my friends and I would drink in there often. I noticed that sometimes other kids—older kids we knew from the neighborhood--were brought into the back room. They'd never talk about what was said back there. It just seemed to be some kind of clandestine operation they were involved with; the bar owners had special "projects" for these kids to complete. Later, in the 1990's, the world found out through news and TV reports that this Tali's Bar was owned by the ill-famed Sammy "The Bull" Gravano, and they had actually murdered one of their own, Michael DeBatt, right in there behind the bar. (Gravano, by his own admission was a hit man for the mob who became Underboss for Mafia Don John Gotti. Gravano eventually turned on Gotti and broke the cardinal rule of the mob by "ratting out" many members in open court to escape justice; he was, at the time, the highest-ranking member of the mob ever to turn government informant. Gravano entered the federal Witness Protection Program; Gotti was sentenced to life in prison, where he died of cancer years later. Sammy "The Bull," incidentally, eventually left the Witness Protection program and returned to a life of crime. Convicted of drug charges, he is currently serving a 19-year-sentence in Arizona State Prison.)

The door to the room I was sitting in suddenly flew open and banged loudly into the wall behind it, which made me jump. The Boss was now here. The big guy who had come up to the roof to get me told him, "Look, this is the prick that stole your car."

48

The Boss got close up near my face and screamed, "You fuck--you're Jerry? You stole my fuckin' car, you son of a bitch!"

"I'm sorry, I didn't mean to," I told him, in a barely audible voice.

"You didn't mean to!?! What the fuck does that mean? How old are you?" he yelled at me.

I mumbled softly that I was seventeen. Tears started welling up in my eyes. I really couldn't play the tough guy because I was scared shitless now. My instincts told me, though, that I'd probably get through this because of my age. I figured that they wouldn't kill a kid just for stealing a car. That would bring too much attention to them.

I didn't know it at the time, but this "boss" was a local bookie--you know, the guy who takes bets on the horses or sporting events illegally. I knew my own dad was a bookie who specialized in the horses and the numbers. When I was about seven years old, he used to take me down to the Brooklyn waterfront, Pier One, where he and my uncles worked unloading ships right near the Brooklyn Bridge. (They were officially known as stevedores.) I'd have to accompany him into the men's room. There I'd see him reaching way behind toilet tanks and up behind lighting fixtures, and then pulling his hand out holding tiny pieces of yellow paper with small--almost illegible--numbers written on them. These were the bets. When I was older he explained to me that the yellow paper was "torch" paper, which meant that if the cops were coming in for a raid, he could put a match to it and it would quickly burst into flames, destroying all evidence that could be used against him in court.

"Where the fuck is my wife's Tupperware?" the Boss started yelling. And now I realized which car it was, that had belonged to the Boss. It was the car that I had used to pick up this girl we called Lori Duck. (So named because she had Daffy Duck's lips.) She and I had gone cruising around in the car.

"I gave it all to my mother" I stuttered.

Before I had dumped the car, I had checked the trunk. To my delight, it was filled with brand new Tupperware-- lots of it. I quickly brought it all home to my mom, filling up the big, old-fashioned wooden cabinets in the kitchen to surprise her. I told her that a friend's older sister was giving it away because she was getting out of the Tupperware Party business.

"Your mother? Yeah, well, I'll tell you what, fuckface-- we're going to your house and you're gonna get it back for me." The Boss paused, shaking his head and looking at the other guys in the room, and said, "Can you believe this little fuck?" The other guys shook their heads, too. The big guy made a "puuu" sound with his mouth.

"Where the fuck are my leisure suits?" the Boss asked. In the '70s, leisure suits were the worst-looking, two-piece polyester pieces of shit you'd ever seen someone wear. Think back to episodes of the TV show "Three's Company" with Suzanne Somers. You may remember that when the homophobic landlord was getting ready for a big date, he'd outfit himself with one of these ghastly ensembles.

Now I was shaking a bit more, knowing that I had to tell him what I had done with his four leisure suits, which were on hangers, in plastic sheathing from the dry cleaners, when I found them. I'd say they were worth a couple of hundred dollars. The Boss wanted them back, now.

I stalled a minute--there was complete silence--and then I very softly said, "I, um, I, ah, threw them out the window."

He started yelling, cursing and waving his hands as he circled around the chair I was sitting in. "You what!?! You threw them out what window? Where? What window? Where the fuck are they?"

While Lori Duck and I were driving around and drinking, I suggested that we go for a ride on the Belt Parkway, the highway that links Brooklyn to Long Island. As we were driving, we wanted to open the windows to feel the rush of air. When we opened the windows though, the wind generated from the high speed at which we were traveling started blowing onto the plastic that was wrapped around the leisure suits. They were hanging on the ceiling hook behind the front driver's seat and started making a racket. I decided to grab them off the hook with my right hand by reaching back over my head, while I drove with my left hand. After I had a grip on them, I flung them onto the back seat. A few minutes later though, the wind once again started to make the plastic ripple wildly. I reached back, picked them up and put them on the front seat, between us, and that did it, the noise stopped. As we sped forward, I now decided that I wanted Lori to slide over toward to me so that I could wrap my right arm around her while I drove. As I struggled yet again to move the leisure suits out of our way, I was having trouble as they were sliding out of my hands. I yelled "fuck this," hollered to Lori to bend her head down and flung them all out of the passenger side window, one by one. I now had to tell "the Boss" that his leisure suits, still wrapped in plastic, were somewhere in Jamaica Bay near Kennedy Airport.

With great trepidation and with the sinking feeling that after I tell him this, I would surely become fish-food, I ever so gently repeated, "I... um...threw them...out the window on the, um, Belt Parkway."

After I admitted that, the Boss flew into a rage. "You hear this shit? Nunzio, is this kid your friend? We should kill this fuck. You hear what he said? My fuckin' leisure suits are on the highway."

Nunzio replied, "Nah, he's not my friend. But I know his mother; I hear he's a good kid."

After a long moment of complete silence, and to my relief, the Boss simply walked out. The other guys followed. I sat there alone. After a few minutes, Nunzio came back in by himself and said, "Come on, Jerry, let's go get the Tupperware from your house."

What had happened--or had almost happened--made me realize that if I truly didn't care about living, all I had to do was continue this kind of behavior. I was sure it wouldn't be long before I'd get a bullet to the head. I really do think my young age saved me that day. Had I been in my 20's, they might have let me have it, or at least threw me a good beating.

A few months later on, when I finally was able to buy an inexpensive used car, I pulled up to the very store where I used to relieve others of their vehicles. I double-parked, and started walking toward the store's front door. And then, out of nowhere, this guy steps right up to my face. It was the Boss.

"Oh, look at this--you got your own car here now. How would ya like now I steal your car from you? Huh? How would you like that? Yeah, gimme the keys; come on, gimme the keys. I'm gonna take your car. We'll see how you like it."

"Please, no; come on, don't do this! I told you that I was sorry. Please!" I begged, not handing him the keys.

At that point, he said, "Oh, I see you have some nice jewelry. Turn around, I'm takin' that fuckin' rope chain." I hesitated, and then reluctantly turned around timidly. He unhooked the clasp holding the expensive 24-carat rope chain that was around my neck. "Oh yeah, this is nice," he said. "Lemme see that ring on your finger. What's that, white gold? Beautiful! Yeah, gimme that ring too. I love white gold." He picked my hand up and slid the ring off of my pinky.

He smiled as he walked away with my jewelry, probably figuring he'd get busted by the cops if he actually took the car. In the end, I guess I got off cheap.

"Saturday Night Fever" Filming Begins!

Spring 1977--Age 18

#1 song on the radio: "Dancing Queen—Abba

The first time I was on a real movie set, I was about 13 years old. We had moved from the Park Slope section of Brooklyn to Bensonhurst a few years earlier. When my mom, my brother Ken and I first got to this new neighborhood, my brother and I were the "outsiders." Other kids were pulling knives on us, and I was getting beat up regularly, both at school and at the playground. To escape this emotional trauma, I secretly started to sniff glue, Carbona (carpet cleaner) and under-arm deodorant after school to get high. It's now known as "huffing" and is reported to be epidemic among teens these days. By age 12, I was also playing guitar and singing in a band, and--like many other kids--I'd fantasize about becoming a "movie star" or something like that. I wanted to be "someone."

The movie *Summer of '42* had been a box-office hit when it was released in 1971, and subsequently, in 1972 they were filming scenes for the sequel, *Class '44,* two blocks from our apartment (This was comedian John Candy's feature film debut.) One of the stars of the film, Jerry Houser, saw me standing for hours near a roped-off area during the shoot and invited me onto the set. It was fascinating to be only steps away from the action and then be invited into the trailer to hang out with the actors. This made quite an impression on me.

Years later, in 1976, *New York Magazine* published an article by British writer Nik Cohn called "Tribal Rites of the New Saturday Night." It was all about the new dance craze called Disco, and the story focused on a small nightclub in Brooklyn called The 2001 Odyssey. Producer Robert Stigwood read the article and quickly decided to make a movie based upon it. They'd be filming in Bay Ridge and Bensonhurst, and shooting the key scenes at the club itself—802 - 64th Street, Bay Ridge, Brooklyn.

Even though I'd go to The 2001 Odyssey a couple of times a month, some other guys and girls in the neighborhood were there several nights a week. Three of those guys that I knew personally were Victor Medina, Gene Pallotto and Eugene Robinson. From what we could all see at that time, though, it was Eugene Robinson who stood out as a dancer; he would be the apparent inspiration for the lead character in the film, "Tony Manero," played by John Travolta (fresh from starring in a hit TV series).

The entire neighborhood went nuts during this heady time. It felt like all of New York—maybe all of America, were fixated on the filming. This was a big picture, representing our lives and times, being made in our own neighborhood. Because of their cooperation during interviews, in the research phase of production, Victor, Gene and Eugene were all given silent bits in the film. And Victor's girlfriend, Carmen, who I also knew well, actually wound up sitting in the lower left-hand corner of that now-famous poster for the movie, showing Travolta wearing his white suit, arm pointed to the heavens. The three guys were able to parlay this instant celebrity they'd attained into some major press, plus occasional club appearances around the region. I heard that Eugene Robinson sued Paramount over their supposedly using him as an inspiration for the "Tony Manero" character, and that they agreed to a cash settlement of $150,000; that was the rumor going around, anyway.

While *Saturday Night Fever* filmed, the entire area around the club became a madhouse. Kids from all different neighborhoods were coming around just to hang out, and see what they could see. Maybe a glimpse of Travolta! There were traffic jams on Eighth Avenue. People were just milling about, soaking it all in. I was one of them.

"Yo, Jerry! Yo, over here!" As I looked through the crowd--at first not being able to see who was shouting my name--there suddenly appeared Stevie Bones rushing toward me. He and I were on the outs lately as he'd started hanging out with a different crew--which was just fine with me. The year before, Stevie and I had done a pretty big money "thing," and then we'd divided up the proceeds between us. Fair enough--except that later, he broke into my family's apartment and stole back my share of the money. Of course he denied doing it, but I knew it was him. I was disappointed in him for turning against me; I hated seeing him disintegrate into a real backstabbing thug. We'd gone through so much together. We'd been shot at, beaten up, and both of us had been physically injured in numerous "scores." No, I wasn't an angel by any means; I know that. But at least I was determined to somehow not stay trapped forever in this horrible, drug-fueled, crime-ridden life.

"Yeah, howya' doin' Stevie?" I replied coldly, with suspicion.

Stevie went on to tell me that I should watch my back because he had seen that there were crews from everywhere hangin' out that day. We both then glanced around and could see the Puerto Ricans from Sunset Park, the Irish kids and Poles from Bay Ridge, some Russian guys from Brighton Beach, and of course different cliques of fellow "Guidos"--Italians like us--all littering the surrounding blocks.

He went on, "Remember that shitty Angel Dust we made? Well, I found out that some of the guys that bought it from us are here--and if they recognize us, they're gonna fuck us up!"

Ah, shit. He was right, and I knew that I should leave right away. *Now!*

The year before, Stevie and I had had the bright idea that we could make our own Angel Dust and then sell it. We were able to buy bottles of formaldehyde—which, as you may know, is used in embalming fluid--from some guy. Someone had casually told us that all we had to do to make Angel Dust was to boil formaldehyde until it was a powder, and then sprinkle it onto oregano. That's what we'd been told, anyway. And we didn't check it out to see if that was accurate. We just figured we could make a lot of money.

After word got out on the street that there was Angel Dust available for sale at our park, cars were lining up left and right for curbside purchases. We were excited

that people were buying our homemade Angel Dust--
even though we'd almost poisoned ourselves making it.
When we had started cooking it, both of us had
accidentally inhaled the noxious fumes and wound up
vomiting and choking violently. But that didn't matter to
us anymore, once we started selling the stuff; business
was brisk.

What we didn't anticipate, though, were the hordes of
dissatisfied customers coming back to look for us hours
later. Yes, we'd inadvertently poisoned everyone! Scores
of people were coming back cursing and yelling, and
saying: "Where are those fucks? They're dead meat!"
Because no one got high off of what we'd sold them--not
even a buzz. What they did get, though, were the worst
debilitating headaches imaginable!

"Awright, awright, I'm leaving now; take care Stevie," I
mumbled. With that I bid Stevie Bones adieu, while my
eyes darted nervously around the large crowd as I left.

The Violence and Mayhem Continue

Again, it was apparent to me that if I didn't make some
serious changes in my life, I was headed for certain
disaster. The fact that I was out there running amok, and
not in prison some place, was perhaps just a matter of
chance.

The penal system in New York during the 1970's was
so overcrowded—so overburdened by the recidivists, the

career criminals—that judges weren't sentencing guys like me to any real jail-time unless we were arrested five or six times, and only then if the arrests were for big crimes. The sentence we'd be given was always "probation." This was truly "turnstile justice" compared to upstate New York or rural New Jersey, where I'd noticed that they'd lock you up quickly for small crimes.

By this time, I'd already seen—however briefly--the inside of the gritty Rikers Island prison complex. There I'd found myself outnumbered by Black and Hispanic inmates—often bigger and older than me--who all seemed to know each other. I didn't want to wind up in there for good.

I was acutely aware back then, that as long as you were under 16 years of age when you were arrested for something, you didn't have to worry too much. Once you reached age 16 though, you were prosecuted as an adult,--even if still rather lightly at first. And that made things riskier. I remember making it a point to remind the other kids of this, as each of them approached their 16th birthday, but they didn't listen and they'd all just laugh at me. The men in the neighborhood often recruited us for assignments, but once I turned 16 years old, I balked. I'm very ashamed to say that the most extreme type of crimes that I was ever involved in, the type that could send you away for much more than just a few years, all occurred before I ever even turned 16 years old.

There were bad things happening everywhere. Some kids were selling machine guns, while others were doing "insurance jobs"—committing arson by using gasoline, with match books serving as homemade timers. There was the usual drug-dealing, that we pretty much took for granted, plus lots of petty armed robberies--although some had by now "graduated" to robbing banks.

Even though Bensonhurst was a violent place for those of us kids who chose that lifestyle, it was--and is-- deceptively well-kept and neat-looking. Having a mob presence there helped keep the neighborhood serene in appearance; it also helped keep the neighborhood safe from outsiders coming in to commit crimes. Those of us who lived in Bensonhurst were busy enough committing our own crimes; we didn't need outsiders.

Well-behaved good kids were not immune to the violence either. A year before, my cousin Ron—who was almost two years my junior and not at all involved with the stuff that I was into--experienced such violence. Oh, he'd go to Tali's Bar and drink a bit sometimes, but he was just really a good kid. Nevertheless, he was viciously stabbed three times by a group of kids who'd verbally disrespected his girlfriend while he tried to stand up for her. They left him for dead; the knife missed his lung by one inch.

It was about this same time that another cousin of mine, Robert--also a kid whose worst offense was simply drinking a bit too much--got stabbed. His stabbing was to the chest, after he and my kid brother Ken had gotten into a fight with some kids. The knife barely missed his heart.

And then, to my disbelief, yet another cousin of mine, Anthony, was stabbed in his own kitchen. And he died from that vicious, bloody attack.

~

"Psst, psst--Ron, Ronnie." I whispered.

Laying there in a hospital bed at Maimonides Hospital in Brooklyn, recovering from being stabbed, was my cousin Ron. Even though it was well after midnight, I'd climbed a fence outside the hospital to enter a restricted area that I could see had an open door to the employee parking lot. Once inside, I marched confidently to the wing, and to the floor that I knew he was on; no one even questioned me!

"Holy shit, what are you doin' here?" Ron replied with a half smile, stunned.

I found it pretty funny that he was lying there reading an edition of *Playboy* magazine in this dark room illuminated only by the small reading lamp on his table.

"I wanted to come visit you," I said. "Wanna smoke a joint?"

Since Ron and I had grown up together and he knew the "real me," he wasn't taken aback by this behavior.

"Ha, ha," I cackled idiotically. "This is some real good shit I got, man." With that, I slid a joint out of my pocket, lit it, and then passed it to him. Here he is, with a tube going into his lung, and now he's puffing on a joint.

"Ha, ha, whattsa matta?" I asked after he started coughing.

I took the joint from him and sucked down the smoke and held it in. After a few seconds, I too started coughing and choking while a cloud of smoke filled the room. Just then we both could hear one of the nurses, out in the hall, yell to the other, "Do you smell that?"

"Shit," I said. I took the magazine off the bed and started fanning the smoke away. We could hear scrambling footsteps in the hallway as the nurses tried to determine which room the smell was coming from.

Figuring that I should hide, I got down on my hands and knees, and crawled under the bed, and stayed still. About a minute later, a nurse came in. As I'm looking at her lower legs from my uncomfortable position, I heard, "Come out from under there right now!" I sheepishly slid out from under the bed with a wise-ass grin on my face and said, "Sorry, I'm just visiting my cousin." We were both surprised and relieved that this nurse was actually very nice about the whole thing. She advised me that I should leave, and that was it. A week later, Ron was released.

You'd Better Work it Girl

It was by sheer luck I hadn't had my own stay at the hospital that year. The Kawasaki motorcycle on which I'd been buzzing around the neighborhood had been destroyed by my sliding under a garbage truck. When I had first gotten the bike, I proudly announced to everyone that I was too smart to ride while I was high. Initially, I was able to adhere to my rule. I'd lock the bike up in the alley of my apartment building, knowing that I was going to be drinking and using drugs that night. But after a while, when I'd be a few hours into my "high," I'd make a beeline for the bike and repeatedly tempted fate by racing around the highways.

What was I going to do for transportation now that my bike was destroyed? I needed to drive. One night I stole a yellow taxi and decided to pick up fares in Manhattan to make some money. People kept giving me locations to drive to and I kept making wrong turns, obviously not knowing where I was going. I'd yell back to them, "Don't worry, I'll take some money off the fare." At one point that night, a suspicious couple frantically swung the door open and jumped out when I stopped for a red light. I shouted to them, "No, it's OK. Come back!" Maybe it had something to do with that little photo of the driver that's posted above the glove box not looking like me?

My friend Johnny Reb had an old white car that didn't have any shocks and that would comically bounce up and down any time he'd come to a stop. It was so ridiculous-looking that when he'd come by the park, all the guys would excitedly run over and start pushing the back bumper down, and then let it go just to watch it bob for fun.

I made a deal with Johnny Reb that if he lent me the car for a few days, I'd put shocks in. He gave it to me and told me that he didn't have the paperwork for it yet. He swore to me that the car wasn't stolen. I believed him.

My steady girlfriend Mary Lou and I were drifting a little bit apart at this time. I knew that her friends detested me for the crowd I was with, and for the reputation that our crowd had. "Who cares?" I thought-- trying to convince myself that it really didn't bother me.

With Johnny Reb's car bouncing up and down at every stop sign--while people were pointing and laughing--I finished chugging down a quart of Colt 45 beer and headed for Mermaid Avenue in Coney Island. Of course I knew from experience that this was a dangerous place to go late at night, but I didn't care; I wanted a hooker.

Just the month before, five of us had traveled to one of the City of New York's public health stations to get free penicillin shots because we'd all contracted VD after one of our wild, late-night escapades in Manhattan. So I should have known better.

It was a weeknight, about 1:30 am, as I slowly made my way along rundown Mermaid Avenue. About a half-dozen prostitutes in glittery clothing swarmed my car as I pulled to the filthy curb, reaching their hands into the open window and down to between my legs, all competing for my dollars. I quickly pointed to the tallest one and asked, "How much?" She replied, got in, and told me that there was a parking lot about seven blocks away near the boardwalk, and directed me toward it.

As we drove down the deserted street, I suddenly froze; for I saw what appeared to be a police car, parked on the side street of the intersection we were just about to go through. Remember--I had no license, and no papers for the car; and sitting next to me was this huge Amazon-like woman with giant hair, clown makeup, and big hoop earrings, who smelled like she'd bathed in perfume. *"Fuck,"* I thought. Plus, the car was bobbing up and down along the pothole-ridden street.

I immediately slowed down, mistakenly slowing too much, which only made us more conspicuous. As we approached the intersection where the police were, I sat up as straight as I could with both hands on the steering wheel, eyes straight ahead, and yelled over to her, "Act natural." With that, we glided quietly past the cop car. I breathed a sigh of relief until I looked in my rearview mirror and could see that the cops were right behind us, their roof mounted spinning red lights illuminating the inside of my car with a slow strobe effect. They motioned to me to pull over. Since I couldn't produce any papers on the car, we were soon joined by a second squad car, and my new "jumbo-sized" girlfriend and I were hauled into the police station.

After we arrived, I was taken into a brightly lit office area where there were several other male and female cops. I guess they were booking the girl in a separate room on a soliciting charge. But when I asked what was going to happen to me, I was told to shut up. A couple of hours passed while I sat there, wondering what was going on. Finally, a couple of cops came into the room, pointing at me and laughing loudly, as if they were at a party or something.

One of the cops announced to me, while slapping another cop on his back, "Hey kid, this is your lucky night in more ways than one." They all broke into uproarious laughter yet again. Finally, one of them said, "OK, now get out of here and don't let us catch you around this area again." They also told me not to drive without the necessary documents in the future.

What I found annoying was that now while they were releasing me, they kept whispering to each other and laughing, and they would do that with each new cop that entered the room. I was getting irritated and started asking, "What, What?" This only caused them to look at each other and laugh even louder. I was thinking, "Friggin' assholes." If it weren't for the fact that I had a roll of counterfeit twenty-dollar bills in my pocket that my crew had been floating in the neighborhood, I would have pushed them for an answer. Fortunately, they hadn't searched me, and I knew I should just get out.

After signing some papers, it was amazing that I was being released with absolutely no tickets or fines, and that I would even be allowed to drive this rocking donkey of a car home, even though I hadn't produced a driver's license! An older cop, who could see that I looked uncomfortable and was perplexed as to why everyone kept laughing, took pity on me.

As he escorted me out of the precinct door and handed me my car keys, he gently said, "Listen, lemme put it to you this way kid. Next time, take a good hard look at the size of her hands and whether or not she has an Adams Apple."

They Came To Rape? And Scarred My Face

Spring 1979--Age 20

#1 song on the radio: "Hot Stuff"—Donna Summer

Feeling weak and unable to break into a full run, I slowly trotted with a sloppy stride--running like one of those actors in the "Planet of the Apes" movies would run, gimpy. It was about 11 o'clock. An extremely dark night; no moonlight, just the familiar, depressing illumination provided by your typical city streetlights. Trying not to panic, I figured if I could just get home and apply some firm pressure to the side of my face with a towel, I could then decide if I needed to go to the hospital for stitches. With every couple of steps that I moved forward, while pressing my left hand to my left cheek, I peeked down to my forearm. By now there were several splintering trails of blood, separate bright red lines running down from my wrist toward my elbow. I thought, "Maybe it's my carotid artery that's bleeding and I'll be dead in a few minutes; I'll never make it home." Panic set in; I started to run faster.

The total distance that I had to make it home from where my face was slashed was one "long" city block. In Brooklyn you have your short blocks and your long blocks, the long blocks being about twice the length of the short blocks. This made for separate rectangular areas throughout the borough that would be jammed packed with thousands of people living within each rectangle. Private houses, two- and three-family houses, apartment buildings, and stores would line the perimeter of the rectangles, with the backs of the different buildings all facing in to each other. That meant if you ever were lucky enough to have a tiny backyard area, you were still always facing the back of someone else's building. I never had a backyard--just an alley, complete with cats, rats, and mice in the garbage-can area. We were lucky enough, though, to have our own clothesline strung across that alley to hang wet clothes. That was great unless a strong wind blew your clothes off the line and--in our buildings case--you had to descend four stories to retrieve them from the dirty alley below. Assuming, of course, that nobody had stolen them yet.

As I continued running, I figured that, at this pace, I could make it home to my apartment building within two or three minutes. Suddenly, when I was about halfway down the block, I heard a familiar female voice yell out from across the street.

"Jerry, look out, behind you!" It was Debbie. She was a pretty brunette who hung out with a different group of kids than I did; I basically only knew her from saying hello over the years. She was out that night with a few girls and guys in front of one of the nicer, private homes across the street. I'd never been invited to "hang" with this particular group because the guys were all goody-two-shoe athletes and my "rep" frightened them. Of course they would never admit to this fear. I'm quite sure that they just dismissed me as just some out of control asshole who was on drugs, nodded in agreement and had all decided to avoid me.

I nervously turned around to see what Debbie was yelling about, while at the same time trying to hold my bloody face with my equally bloody hand. It was the Puerto Rican girl known as Nilda, wildly waving a very large kitchen knife that looked to me like the one Norman Bates used in the movie "Psycho."

"I kill you, I kill you, you fuck; I kill you!" she yelled in a thick Spanish accent as she rushed toward me. She had blood on her face and arms. As I tried to run from her, I felt not fear but rage toward her. After all, I had just tried to protect her from being attacked--and now she was trying to stab me!

Circling around a parked car to escape her, I kept yelling to her that I had actually been trying to help her back there; but she wouldn't listen. She was hysterical--screaming and crying. And, perhaps most scary of all, she was clearly drunk. In my experience with people drunk or on drugs, that meant that she could have actually plunged that butcher knife into my back and killed me. I told myself, "Get the fuck out of here!" And I kicked my running into high gear.

Let me give you some background. Nilda was pretty new to the neighborhood. I was one of the first people in our area to meet her; she didn't seem to know anyone else in the neighborhood but me. And she and I were the same age. She lived with her grandmother in the multi-family apartment building on the corner. And her grandmother worked nights in a factory--from midnight to eight in the morning.

Although I never considered myself Nilda's boyfriend--nor did she consider herself my girlfriend; we talked about these things--I spent many nights at her apartment while her grandmother was at work. (Again, this was during one of the many periods that my regular girlfriend and I were on the outs.) In the mornings, I would scurry out of there before Nilda's grandmother got home from work.

To me, Nilda seemed a bit mysterious, though. She would disappear during the day, just saying that she had to go to Manhattan where her family was. When I'd meet up with her during the evening, she always had lots of money and was very generous with it. This was fun for a while, so I went along with it.

Many mornings, I'd be awakened by the annoying sound of her hair dryer as Nilda went through her daily hairdo, make-up, and clothing routine. I used to comment to her that between her flashy way of dressing and her liberal dousing of designer perfume, which I loved, she might someday be mistaken for a hooker-- which I later found out is exactly what she was.

During a drunken conversation with Nilda one night, she leaked just enough information for me to conclude that she actually was a hooker. Upon confronting her with the question, she offered no resistance. Well, that was it! I was out of there. It's funny, because even though I'd always kept an emotional wall up between us—even though I'd never wanted a real relationship with her--I felt lied to, betrayed. This was about four years before any of us heard of AIDS, so AIDS, specifically, was not a concern for me. But I felt that she could have transmitted some kind of STD to me. I mean, most of the time that I was with her I used a condom; but not always.

A few weeks later, after I had stopped seeing Nilda, I guess my gross immaturity, as well as my anger towards her, allowed me to spew details of what had happened between she and I to the guys in my main crew. That included Junior, Philly, Vinnie, Mikey T. and Stevie Bones. A couple of other, younger kids, about seventeen years old –Jo Jo and Butchie—also happened to be there while I was telling the story.

Jo Jo and Butchie both looked up to Junior, and wanted to "prove their worth" in the neighborhood by doing crazy shit. I noticed though that these kids could only "perform" while under-the-influence. To me, they had no real balls, because they needed to be high to pull anything off. They were wannabes.

Telling everybody about Nilda was a big mistake; I should have known better. But this was an ongoing problem of mine. I'd get high and I'd sometimes shoot off my mouth. This was a definite no-no in that neighborhood and a guarantee that I'd never get any kind of ranking with the mob guys. I only acted like this if I was high. The problem was that I was always high.

A couple of nights later, when they were as drunk and high and as rowdy as any gang could get, they made their way over to her place. I wasn't there when they decided to head to her apartment. I'd been over in Bath Beach that night. When I got back to the park, where we all usually hung out, I asked some people where my guys were. They said they'd heard that the whole bunch of them—really fucked up on pills and liquor--were going to see some Puerto Rican whore. And I knew what that meant. *Shit. Nilda.*

I was fearful for Nilda of what those guys might be capable of. There'd been rumors of some of them being involved in the gang rape of a girl. I never questioned them about this and wasn't even sure if it were true. At the very least, I knew they'd harass her and also knew that while they were in that state of mind, anything could happen, and it'd be my fault.

It was six short city blocks down and one long city block over to get to the building where Nilda lived. I had to get there as fast as I possibly could.

Out of breath, I arrived in the small courtyard in front of her building. I was relieved to see most of the guys still outside the locked vestibule doors, hovering around the intercom-buzzer panel. Somehow, they had gotten her grandmother's last name, and now they were ringing Nilda's bell over and over, demanding that she buzz them in. I could hear her voice, crackling and distorted from the faulty intercom speaker, cursing them and threatening to call the cops.

I yelled, "What the fuck are you doin' here?" I could see that every one of them were wasted. They were definitely on Tuinals or Seconal, the "gorilla biscuits." When those guys were high on barbiturates, there was no talking sense to them. They were loud, violent, and determined. They were out to terrorize.

"Fuck you, Castaldo!" Butchie yelled almost incoherently.

"Yeah, go fuck yourself," Junior chimed in. Butchie was hoping to look good in front of everyone by disrespecting me right there out in the open. I'm sure he thought this would make him look tough, fearless.

I heard the sound of breaking glass, then screaming, then more breaking glass and banging. I now realized that Junior had instructed Stevie, Philly and Vinnie to go around the back alley to her window, which was at street level. I guessed that they had found it because they knew the apartment number from the buzzer panel. Only later did I learn that Nilda's hands and arms were cut from fending them off through the broken rear windows.

"You fuckin' assholes, the cops will probably be here any minute; you better take off now!" I yelled at the top of my voice.

Butchie yelled back belligerently, "Fuck you, Naldo!"-- inventing on the spot what he thought was his own humorous variation on my last name.

I forcefully pushed the palm of my hand up against his face as I ran toward him and yelled, "Come on, muthafucka."

By now, people's heads were popping out of various windows of the apartment building. And I could hear that the guys in the back alley were now indiscriminately breaking any windows in the building that they could, yelling and laughing like lunatics. Butchie got into a fighting stance, both fists raised up ready to box me. I threw a few punches, he threw a few punches. The other guys out in front of the building with us started to run away from the scene. It was just me and him now, and I knew that there'd be a cop car pulling up any second.

We exchanged a few more punches until a round-house from him connected to the left side of my head, by my left ear. We kept bobbing and weaving while people were starting to come out of the lobby. Then, abruptly, Butchie stopped fighting, looked at me kind of startled, and turned around and ran away. I didn't understand it until I felt the warm sensation of blood on my cheek.

"Hey kid—you're bleeding bad; you better get to a hospital," some guy walking his dog offered.

I don't know if it was due to plain stupidity or my absurd machismo, but when I got home I decided not to go to the hospital for treatment. My life-long sentence for this mistake has been fielding endless questions from people I continue to meet in adulthood who wonder, "Where did you get that scar on your face?" I don't think it would have become a raised scar if it had been stitched properly. Butchie had hidden an opened box-cutter inside his fist, and when he connected with his punch, the razor had ripped into my ear, slicing a half-inch slit clean through and out the back of my ear. The razor blade had then swept down, over my earlobe--cutting but not severing it--and continued slicing two more inches down the sideburn-area toward my check.

The only comfort I took from that evening was knowing that I'd kept them away from Nilda. And knowing that in a mere five days I'd be on a plane, heading out of Brooklyn for at least three years.

A month earlier, a gang of guys in several different cars had come by my apartment building looking for me. They had yelled at my neighbors, threatening them and demanding they give me a message: "Tell Jerry he's dead." Of course, because of who I hung out with, I had no clue as to what I was supposed to have done. I might have been targeted because of something that I wasn't even involved with.

I can tell you this, though--that particular day is when I decided that there could be a whole new life for me, a reprieve from the madness; a chance for a new direction and beginning.

Marching very deliberately up to the 18th Avenue US Army recruiting office, which was next door to "Sammy The Bull's" place, Tali's, on the very next day after I had gotten that death threat, I asked the Sergeant, "How far away can you send me?"

He replied, "Germany or South Korea."

I confidently, loudly, and clearly told him, "Germany! Where do I sign, and when can I leave?"

Escape to US Army Basic-Training

Summer 1979--Age 20

#1 song on the radio: "Ring My Bell"—Anita Ward

"You look like ya wanna hit me, Private Castaldo. Do ya wanna hit me? Do you think you're some kind of 'Mafia,' Private Castaldo? Mafia from New York? C'mon on, boy, hit me, hit me! Aw, you ain't no Mafia from New York, Private Castaldo; you is just a sorry-ass faker. You don't even have the balls to stand up for yourself. C'mon, hit me; do it now!"

These taunts were being screamed into my face ferociously, at full volume, by the Drill Sergeant as I stood at attention on the dirt road outside the mess hall. I could smell his breath, and I could feel his spittle hit my face as he yelled. His "good ole boy" southern drawl reminded me that I was very far from home.

Only six weeks before, I had been sneaking in and out of my Brooklyn apartment building to avoid the carloads of guys that kept coming to look for me, so they could "throw me a beating." (For what, I still don't know.) Now, I was nearing the end of what I felt was my very successful completion of US Army basic-training. My very first airplane ride, courtesy of the US Government, had delivered me to the sprawling Fort Jackson Army Base in South Carolina for eight weeks of combat training.

With only a couple of weeks to go, this drill sergeant was doing to me what I guess they are supposed to do-- break down people to see who can't handle the intense pressure. This way, they can be discharged now rather than "losing it" in combat, and endangering the lives of other soldiers. Even though I knew and understood this, and had played the game well so far, I *did* want to hit him. He was trying to terrorize me; he was abusing me. My street instincts kicked in, and my natural defense mechanism sizzled. I knew this feeling. My breathing became labored, my legs and arms started to twitch; I could feel my entire body start to tremble. I could feel my eyes getting watery. All I kept saying to myself was: *"This isn't real; he's only playing with you. You'll get discharged and sent back to Brooklyn if you hit him. Don't do it. It'll all be a total waste if you put your hands on him; you will fail."*

We've all seen this on television and in the movies--the familiar scenes of young recruits being pushed to their mental, physical, and emotional limits. I reminded myself that, when I enlisted, I couldn't wait for this training to start. I had wanted this. I'd wanted the structure, the discipline, the chance to get out of New York and build my mind, body, and spirit; the chance to finally get away from the street cronies. If I could just get through basic training, and then another eight weeks of specialty schooling, I'd be off for Europe.

Up until this point, I actually had been kind of enjoying the intense challenges. Believe it or not, I found it fun getting up at 4:30 am to run five miles with dozens of other soldiers, then somehow making it through a full 19-hour day before we'd retire for a short five-hour sleep. It was different and it was exciting. I didn't want to blow it now by losing my temper.

"You think you're such a tough guy with that scar on your face, don't you, Private Castaldo?"

I could hardly get the words out: "No, Drill Sergeant."

It had only been a week before I left for basic training that I'd had my left ear and cheek slashed with a box cutter by one of the neighborhood guys, so I had great difficulty shaving every morning. Only cold water was available, and our hurried pace kept causing me to knock off the scab, so the slash wasn't healing correctly; it would continue to bleed, week after week. Couple that with the rumors of how I supposedly got the bloody looking tear in my cheek, my Italian last name, my heavy Brooklyn accent, and my thoroughly ingrained macho street swagger, and this drill sergeant had all the ammo he needed to push my buttons.

He continued: "You ain't shit, Private Castaldo. Why would I want you in my Army?"

After our early morning runs in the dark, we would then stand in formation at Parade Rest, our feet shoulder-width apart, elbows bent with our hands open flat and layered onto the small of our backs, eyes straight ahead. We'd stay like that for up to one hour sometimes, waiting completely motionless outside the mess hall before we'd get in and on line for chow. The sweat from our run would soak our hair and uniforms. And it could get a bit chilly standing out there, soaked in sweat, particularly if clouds obscured the morning sun. (I laughed the first time I heard chattering teeth during this formation; it reminded me of the battery operated, chattering novelty toy-teeth they used to sell during the Halloween season.)

The reason I was being berated with such intensity by the drill sergeant this day was because of a big, boisterous scene I had made while in line inside the mess hall. Maybe that morning I was more tired than usual, but all I can really remember is seeing—as I stood on line in the mess hall, waiting to be served, cafeteria style--that there was only one egg omelette left on the server's tray. After that omelette was gone, it looked like the only thing left to eat would be this disgusting oatmeal that they were serving up, using ice-cream scoops.

The old fashioned, wooden mess hall, which looked like it had been built during WWII, was divided into two sections. One small section, with a tiny cluster of tables, was for the officers; and the other larger section, with many long tables, was for the trainees. We were not allowed to talk--no speaking at all, either outside the mess hall or inside. While standing on line, if you did have to communicate something to the staff, you did so in hushed tones. So, it was very quiet in there--solemn, I'd say--except for the clinking of dishes, glasses, and silverware. Even the officers kept their conversations to a whisper.

When I got to the guy who doled out the omelettes, I motioned submissively while dropping my head down like a Geisha, and eked out, "I'll take the egg omelette." He immediately shot me this dirty look as if to say, "I'll decide what you get." He dropped his spatula, picked up an ice-cream scoop, and deposited what looked like a giant ball of snot onto my dish. He then handed my dish back to me and grinned, looking very satisfied.

I don't know why, but I felt so deprived and victimized that I didn't know how to react. For a moment, I felt like a little kid being denied a toy; I felt like breaking down and crying. But then my feelings quickly morphed into blind rage. I knew I couldn't talk back. I knew I had to keep the line moving. I continued forward for a few steps. I picked up my napkins, my silverware, my glass of milk; I turned and was about to make my way to one of the long tables to sit and eat what I could now smell wafting up from the tray I was carrying ---cooked snot!

Before I could reach the table though, I felt a strong, overbearing compulsion to stop. All I remember was thinking, *"Fuck it!"* I turned around to face the server-- my nemesis. And I stiffly walked in a bee-line directly back to him. The other trainees around me, along with some of the sergeants at the special tables, noticed me going in the wrong direction. Everybody seemed to realize that something was out of whack. I was now in a crazed state, and I'm sure that my eyes reflected that clearly!

As I reached the counter area, I quickly raised my tray up as high as my face with a herky-jerky movement. I could feel the weight of it, as it was now loaded with dishes, glasses and eating utensils. As I yelled at the top of my lungs, "You Mutha Fuckaaa," I forced the full tray down to the floor with all the might I could muster. This resulted in a horrendous crash that shook the entire mess hall and silenced all other sounds. No one said a word. Everybody stopped moving entirely; all eyes were now nervously looking at me, waiting for my next move. I broke protocol and stormed out of the mess hall, slamming the cheap wooden screen door open. I jumped down the wooden steps to make my way up the hill back to the barracks. A drill sergeant from another company, whom I'd seen around but didn't know, ran up after me. I'd heard he was one of the tougher ones, and when he ordered me to stop and stand at attention, I did.

While the drill sergeant kept yelling into my face, I knew that the decision I made at this moment could change my life for good or bad. *Relent, admit I'm wrong, and take the punishment--that would be my salvation. The US Army would be my family away from home, and provide me with food, shelter and a paycheck. To let my street instincts--my phony, bullshit "street pride"--take over, and go ballistic on this guy now, would only put me back on the streets of Bensonhurst....* I did not want that.

So I took my punishment--lots of extra duty involving cleaning--and soon graduated. That drill sergeant from the other company actually shook my hand at graduation. Since my next eight weeks of training were on the other side of the same base, I'd occasionally see him herding new trainees off the bus, and a few times we even talked like regular guys, soldier to soldier.

For me, completing basic training and now heading into the second phase of training (where you actually learn a skill), was a big accomplishment. I was proud of myself. Especially when I think of it now, since some of my biggest regrets in life are not continuing high school past the ninth grade, and not going to college. The Army, I told myself at that time, would be my "college."

Never did I imagine that only nine short months later, while stationed in Germany, I'd be in an Army jail cell, standing on top of a toilet bowl, with one end of my belt wrapped tightly around my neck, and the other end tied above me to a pipe running along the ceiling--trying to decide when would be the "right" moment to allow my feet to slide off.

Phase II of Basic Training

"Good luck and much success to you in the Army, Jerry!" These were the words that my family and friends had echoed to me during the modest "going away" party they had thrown for me after I decided to enlist.

Of course some of my so-called "friends," whom I've described previously-- who weren't really friends at all, but were more like pack members--didn't want me to go, lest I weaken the pack. They laughed and chided me: "The fuckin' *Army*, Jerry? Whatta you crazy?" That's all I heard from them.

As far as I could tell, though, joining the Army was the best thing I could do. I'd seen others from the neighborhood go in and out of jail repeatedly, or die violently. I couldn't remain entrenched in my lifestyle, in Brooklyn, indefinitely. And there just didn't seem to be any other way out. There wasn't any money for me to just move somewhere and start my life over. Of the many jobs that I'd had—and I once counted over 20--all were minimally paying.

As excited and hopeful as I initially was, my dreams had quickly started to fade on the day back when I was set to "in-process" at the Fort Hamilton Army Base in Brooklyn and leave for basic training. My mom, my brother and I all loaded into the old Pontiac Bonneville that was now fourteen years old, still blowing blue smoke, and labeled the scourge of the neighborhood by my wise-ass friends. After we had arrived at the base, all of the people ready to leave for basic training were given dot-matrix-typed "orders," specifying the base you were going to and the MOS—Military Occupation Specialty-- you were going to train in after the basic training. Since I was eager for action and thrills, I had signed up for the famous 82nd Airborne Unit based in Fort Bragg, NC. This elite airborne infantry division was organized in 1917 and its motto, "All The Way," was inspiring to me. I figured: *Why not jump out of planes and learn advanced hand-to-hand combat?*

To my dismay, though, I now saw that my printed orders said: "71 Lima, Administrative Assistant." *What? What is this shit? What is an administrative assistant and what does that entail?*

After taking my papers to someone in charge and having him confirm that yes, indeed, that was what my MOS was, I panicked. I was not going to leave now. *How can they do this to me? This is classic bait-and-switch!*

The man who was checking this out took the matter to another supervisor, who then sat me down and informed me that I could not be assigned to the 82nd Airborne and become a paratrooper because I was color-blind. I protested! *How could the Army agree to my original*

MOS, and then change it at the last minute just when I'm about to fly out? Why didn't they tell me? What was I going to do?

I couldn't believe this! I had already had my going-away party. I had people from my neighborhood who were looking for me, to hurt me; I didn't have any viable prospects here at home. I had to stay in the Army.

But what a punk I was gonna be! Instead of jumping out of a plane and carousing with hard-core soldiers, I was going to be working in an office, like a secretary. *Where's the glory in that? How fucked up is this? I mean, how many war movies do you see the hero bashing his typewriter into the enemy's face?* This truly sucked. But, I kissed my mother and hugged my brother, who'd come to see me off, and I had said goodbye. I was now, as the paperwork said: "Pvt. E1 Jerry Castaldo."

Only during the following month did I learn the truth. The Army had decided that since I had scored so well on the entrance exam (despite my lack of virtually any high school), they didn't want to waste my raw brain power in an infantry unit when they could better utilize me in administration. So, they switched my MOS and never told me until I was in-processing. That was devious of them, but it eventually turned out to be very beneficial for me when I was deployed to my unit in Europe. I also found that, yes, I do have a slight color-blindness problem, but not to the degree that it would have prevented me from reading maps. They "got over" on me-- our Brooklyn street slang for getting fucked.

After you've finished basic training and start the second phase of training (where you learn your skill), you are given many more privileges. After dinner, for example, you actually have free time to do what you want, wear any type of clothing you want, or go off base if you want to. It's not the prison that basic training was. Yeah, you still have to attend formation in the morning to run with the entire company, but not as early. I had friends from my basic-training unit that were now part of the new unit, too, so that was fun. All in all, it was much better at this point. But you had to earn this status. There were many trainees who were discharged during basic training for not keeping up with the program. I also remember hearing that we lost one trainee in another company to heat exhaustion and yet another to an errant bullet discharged from an M16 rifle during a firing-range exercise.

Sometimes things have a funny way of working out for the best. I mean, if it weren't for the US Army lying to me and forcing me into taking that MOS, I wouldn't have the skills to sit here and actually type these stories at a reasonable pace. I really don't think I'd be writing this book myself if I was "hunting and pecking" on a computer keyboard. That said, it still did prove a bit embarrassing later when I had to admit to people back home that no, I hadn't been parachuting from the skies during exciting training missions. It was also tough for me when I'd occasionally run into the elite soldiers from those airborne units. The stories that they told would sound so much more interesting than what I was doing.

"What is this, Private Castaldo? Well, well, now lookie here; we've got a writer, an author, a journalist--ha, ha!"

I was a bit worried to have been caught typing my own thing and not what I was assigned to do. In my typing class there were about 40 male and female soldiers, plus our proctor--the sergeant--who would assign the exercises we had to do. If we wanted to pass the final exam for this class, we would have to be able to maintain a typing speed of 25 words-per-minute, using the correct fingers and keys, without looking at the keyboard. On this particular, day we were supposed to be typing the words: "Mary had a little lamb, his fleece was white as snow..." That is not what I was typing.

"OK, class--stop what you are doing, because now I'm going to read for you what our resident writer, Private Castaldo, has prepared for us. Oooh, this looks juicy. Ready everybody?"

He was mocking me in public. To tell you the truth, though, I really wasn't that embarrassed. I instinctively knew that this would garner me accolades, not ridicule. Half the people I had met in Fort Jackson were already fascinated by me just for the fact of where I was from. So many people that I hung around with were from very small towns.

"Okay class, here's the title: 'The Limitation of The FBI on Organized Crime in NYC.'"

I gulped and held my breath as he read the mish-mash that I had culled from the past weeks' newspapers. Coming from a mob neighborhood had gotten me into reading about organized crime and the various characters involved in that lifestyle. Well, I was always interested in that. I was fascinated, for example, by the fact that my own father had been born on the same exact block--on Garfield Place in Brooklyn--as the notorious gangster Al Capone. I actually used to visit Capone's old headquarters, at the corner of Union Street and Fourth Avenue, and stand outside and look in through the windows of the building. Of course, this was many years after Capone had died of cardiac arrest in 1947 at his Palm Island estate in Miami Beach.

Then there was my father's job on the Brooklyn waterfront, and his association with the International Longshoremen's Union, or ILA for short. Some of my uncles were also gritty dockworkers. (You can go back to the Academy Award-winning film "On the Waterfront" if you want to see how brutal the mob was, and get a sense of its influence on the shipping trade in NY Harbor.) The strong union that the dock workers have does ensure many good things for them; without the union, they'd be slaving at a dangerous job for nothing. The union also provided an ILA Medical Clinic for all workers and their family members. My dad's best friend lost his toes one day, and many others lost their lives, doing this thankless work on the docks. My father's brother--my "Uncle Fat," as we called him--was once involved in a violent Wildcat strike; after trying to stand in front of one of the trucks bringing in "scabs" to do the work of the striking longshoremen, he was run over and crippled for life. He needed the help of a wheelchair until his death.

Was there some mob involvement with that union? Sure. To this day, one of the weirdest things that I remember in connection with the union, is that in the outer hallway of the ILA Medical Clinic in Brooklyn there was a big bronze plaque with a man's image on it. Now, usually when you see something like this, the person depicted on the plaque is some sort of prominent public servant or philanthropist-- someone you're supposed to look up to.

Well, this plaque displayed a carved image of Anthony Anastasio, little brother to infamous gangster Albert Anastasio, who I had mentioned to you earlier.

That's right, there's a plaque there honoring the kid brother of a ruthless killer nicknamed "The Executioner." Anthony became VP of the ILA after following his older brother into organized crime. (Now that I think of it, this may explain why-- when I once had to have some dental work done here at this clinic--the dentist himself looked like a dock worker, wearing short sleeves exposing his big, hairy arms. And smoking a cigarette before he got started on me. When he informed me that he was going to pull one of my teeth, he had two other gangster-looking guys come in and hold me down; I kicked that round tray with the dentist's tools right up into the air. I just remember a lot of pain; they didn't even use enough Novocaine! Tough doctors at that clinic.)

What the sergeant was reading to the class now—my little write-up--was much more interesting than the nursery rhymes we were supposed to be typing. I had started to write this story about Carmine Galante, an East Coast mobster who was gunned down a few months prior in Rosemary's Restaurant in Brooklyn. A bunch of different newspapers had shown the photo of his bloody body, cigar clenched in his teeth, right there in black and white. (I'm sure that some of today's newspapers would think twice about printing such graphic stuff.) In my writing, I was just theorizing on why the FBI seemed not to be able to wipe out organized crime. Writing about the mob interested me--and now I was hoping my writing was interesting to the class.

The sergeant continued reading the five hundred or so words that I had hammered out on the then-cutting-edge-technology IBM Selectric typewriter. What I distinctly remember, though, is the reaction of not only the class, but also of the sergeant himself, after he finished reading what I'd written. Everyone applauded. My written words had sparked an emotional reaction. I was hooked.

The sergeant then instructed the class to settle down, wiped the friendly look right off of his own face, walked toward me and said sternly, as he handed my papers back to me, "I want you to stay with the class, and only type what you're supposed to be typing." Even though the tone in the room had now turned serious, I could still see a twinkle in his eye as he handed me the papers.

I could almost hear him saying, "Good job, Castaldo; you've got a bright future ahead of you, kid."

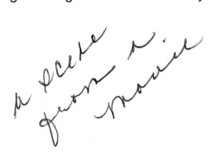

Jerry Castaldo

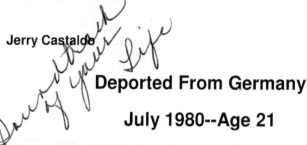

Deported From Germany

July 1980--Age 21

#1 song on the radio: It's Still Rock and Roll to Me—Billy Joel

"Child is born with heart of gold, way of the world makes his heart grow cold..."

That song lyric from the band Earth Wind and Fire will always resonate deeply within me.

Children come into this world pure and untouched--a blank canvas, and an amazing miracle of life. But even with an avalanche of love and with their family guiding them the best they can, there's a risk of them being influenced negatively by their environment.

Fortunately, people can and do change.

The Flight from Brooklyn to Germany

My basic training and advanced MOS training were complete, I'd come home for a final visit before my stint was to begin in Europe, and it was now time for me to fly transatlantic for the very first time in my life. It was the fall of 1979.

All the while that I was home preceding my departure, I'd kept my eyes open for the guys whom I had to assume were still looking for me. I was glad to be leaving for such a long time. I guessed that by the time I

90

did finish my tour and came back, they'd either be dead, in jail, or would have grown up and decided to let bygones be bygones.

I was scheduled to depart from Kennedy International Airport in Queens, NY. The seven-hour-and-twenty-minute flight would be non-stop to Frankfurt, where I'd have to spend one week in-processing. On the day before leaving, I thought to myself that this nighttime flight across the Atlantic Ocean would be more fun if I could somehow find a way to smoke a few joints while airborne. So, I packed some pot. Yeah, one last time-- my last hurrah before I do an about-face, start my new life and get sober. This Boeing jet was one of those mammoth, double-decker planes with hundreds of seats, and that night every one of them was filled.

As I exited the plane's tiny bathroom, amidst a cloud of swirling smoke, there was the distinct aroma of burning marijuana. This made for an absolutely ridiculous scene. The three people waiting in line for the bathroom glared at me with contempt. And what was I doing? Laughing. The flight attendants were not amused. After making my way back to my window seat--smirking as I noticed seated passengers looking around as the smell wafted through the cabin--I drifted off to sleep. Later, after we had landed and I was thinking a bit more clearly, I reflected with surprise that no one had confronted me about my turning the airplane restroom into an "opium den" 20,000 feet up between continents.

Upon entering the Frankfurt Airport, I was taken aback by something that I had never seen in the US. There were German police gripping automatic machine guns, poised and at the ready, deployed throughout the huge, bustling terminal. I reasoned that this must be common in European countries since many of them had dealt before with terrorism--something that we in the United States had been fortunate enough to escape up until that time. As I made my way through a guarded checkpoint, I was relieved that I had finished up all of the pot on the plane; I wouldn't want to be entering this country with it.

I would very soon experience first-hand just how serious the German police were about law enforcement.

~

Finally, here I was, alone. No friends, no family, no familiar sights or faces. This was my chance to break away. To rebuild myself, improve my mind, body, spirit and fulfill all of my dreams. To return to America successful, drug and alcohol free. Things felt promising.

The US Army in-processing facility at Frankfurt proved a bit worrisome to me at first. None of the military personnel who were ordering me around had any kind of personality. They were cold, robot-like, humorless. I was to reside in a solitary room at this complex for a full week while all of the necessary paperwork was completed. I was to do nothing but wait. The weather stayed dark and dreary for the entire time--damp and cold, which only added to the disconnected, weird feeling I was experiencing. Remember-- there was no Internet, email or even inexpensive international phone-calling available at that time. Isolation enveloped me.

But hold on a minute! Wasn't this my "new beginning?" So I decided to start my transformation immediately. I started jogging around the compound twice a day and spent hours in the library reading psychology books. I started to feel better.

The following week I was finally shipped out to the town of Landstuhl, about an hour's ride southeast from the Frankfurt Airport. This small, idyllic-looking municipality, on the edge of the Palatinate Forest, is the site of the Landstuhl Medical Center, a major US Army Hospital. All through the time I was stationed in Landstuhl, I'd see helicopters swooping in, day and night, transporting patients from all over the region in to this then modern facility.

I never imagined that, months later, I would be detained and medicated against my will in the psychiatric ward of this very hospital.

The actual military installation in Landstuhl sits high upon a mountaintop, 814 feet above the town and the medical center. As I sat on an Army transport bus, slowly climbing a steep, winding road to the base, I thought about how lucky I really was that the Army had pushed me into my MOS. By working as an administrative assistant, I was deployed to work in an NCO Academy, which is a school for new sergeants.

Most Private E1's entering the military live in large, nondescript barracks with hundreds of other soldiers.

They have to eat in a huge mess hall, get up early every morning to run in formation, and then do some sort of cleaning duty before they ever even start their regular workday. Since I was now technically part of a Cadre, or teaching staff, I was given a private room of my own right there in the Academy. I did not have to get up and run, nor did I have to clean the facility; the NCO candidates took care of that. Every morning at seven, I would simply walk down a flight of stairs to the basement and report for work. My hair didn't have to be super-short, military style, as long as it did not go over my ears. Every seven weeks, when we were getting ready for a new batch of candidates to arrive and the building was empty, I was even allowed to wear civilian clothes at work for a week. Not bad.

I certainly did have a plush job compared to the average new recruit.

However, substance addiction always has a way of tricking you into justifying what is "OK" for you to do. At first things were going pretty well for me; I was adjusting to my new life. Although I was now free of doing any kind of "hard drugs," I was soon introduced to the black, sticky, tar-like hashish that was very popular over there at that time. Since I knew some soldiers who were shooting heroin, I naively persuaded myself that drinking and smoking hash wasn't all that bad, so long as I kept it under control. They were real addicts, I struggled to convince myself; I was not.

~

On November 4th, 1979 a group of Islamic students took over the American Embassy in Iran in support of the

Iranian revolution. Fifty-two U.S. diplomats that were stationed there were taken hostage. And with a jolt, I realized that I could now wind up serving in the military during wartime. Since I was part of the 92nd Army Air Defense, we were subject to surprise practice drills and alerts; we had to be ready at a moment's notice should we need to be shipped off into conflict.

I remember upping my running schedule and doing more hills to build extra strength, and also trying to prepare myself for war by inventing exercises to improve my reaction time. In one, I'd stand in an open field and fling rocks up and behind me, as far as I could throw them; and then, after hearing them land, I'd quickly turn around while trying to focus on exactly where I thought the rocks were landing. Seems dumb to me now; but at that time, I thought that this would improve my chances of surviving.

Although this international crisis was looming, I finalized plans with my girlfriend Mary Lou to visit me during the Christmas holiday. She flew into Frankfurt, I picked her up, and during her two-week stay, we had fun and were able to visit several countries together.

While she was there, she reminded me of the ongoing pandemonium that continued back in the old neighborhood. Reaching into her luggage, she produced a newspaper article about some guy who shot someone in the back of the head while the victim was crouching down tying his shoelace. An out-and-out execution.

I took the article from her, and there in a large black-and-white photo, handcuffed with his hands in front of him while being led to a waiting car by two grim-looking, dark-suited detectives, was Sal Fezzo. I remembered "Crazy Sal," as he was known to us, as a grammar-school bully, just one year ahead of me. When I was twelve-years old, he slammed a thick glass soda bottle three times over my head, while my brother Ken stood by helplessly. Sal and I fought again after that, too, although we eventually wound up on speaking terms.

I read the entire newspaper story with great interest. I was perplexed by the sheer senselessness of the shooting. I figured that Sal would be in prison for the rest of his life. I never could have imagined that he and I would confront each other again the following year!

I was glad to spend the holidays with Mary Lou. But then she left Germany and returned to the States. After four months of having had no real contact with anyone from back home, it was tough for me to see her go.

Arrested On the Drive Back from Paris

"Yeah, I heard about you people, you fuckin' hate Americans right? Well fuck you all you French motherfuckers!"

My verbal tirade was cut short by two huge bouncers who appeared out of nowhere and started pulling at my arms.

"Keep your hands off me. I'm not doin' nothin'. What about them? They started it." I said.

The taller one sternly said "Let's go." I slammed down some Francs onto the table of the Parisian dance club I was at, and was escorted to the door and out onto the shiny cobblestone street. It was after 1 am on a Sunday morning and raining heavily. I started walking with a shaky gait toward my car.

It was usually fun and exciting for me to drive the 240 miles to Paris on weekends. I loved meeting new people and exploring. But this night had turned out differently. I hadn't been looking to fight with that group of French people at the club, but I'd felt snubbed and had become belligerent because I was in the throes of heavy drinking again. We'd been seated at a large table, enjoying lively conversation. But then, some of them rudely started talking to each other in French and motioning to one another dramatically. Several times their comments culminated in uproarious laughter as they shot looks in my direction. I was convinced that they were making disparaging remarks about me.

It's ironic. I had come all the way from the US to Germany to get away from trouble. And now, because I had gotten in so much more trouble at the local clubs around Landstuhl, Germany, I needed to get away from there, too—going all the way to France. It seemed like I was always running to some new place hoping for a fresh start. But because of what I later learned to be a disease--my addictions-- the outcome was always the same: disappointment. Even though my intentions were good, I'd always relapse and spiral downward.

For a while I was doing pretty well. I was drinking again, but--I told myself--I was not drinking "to excess." I performed with the USO at several locations, singing and playing guitar, and I also traveled to Stuttgart to audition for a play. I was glad I was doing those sorts of things. Another one of my goals--now that I was away from New York--was to get back to my music, and to performing. Before my teen years, I had loved performing with my brother (who played accordion), and I was a member of several different bands. But by the time I was 15 years old and hanging out with a different crowd, I would have looked like a "pussy" if they knew I was into that. So, in order to appear "tough," I stopped all creative expression. Now, in Europe, I didn't feel the need to worry anymore about ridicule.

What *was* discouraging to me back then, though, was chronic, severe pain and clicking in my jaw when I would try to sing. A doctor diagnosed me as having Temporomandibular Joint Dysfunction, or TMJ, as a result of my face being beaten with the hammer. He insensitively announced that I'd never be able to sing properly. Sometimes, for me, it felt like nothing would ever really go right.

Well, there I was—left by the bouncers outside of that Parisian dance club. Another night was ruined. Despite the fact that I was thoroughly inebriated, I decided then to drive back to the base. And that was just plain stupid.

The German Autobahn is a huge highway with an advisory speed of 130 kilometers per hour, or 80 miles per hour, but there is no general speed limit. My five-speed, standard-shift Opel could get up to about 110 mph before I'd feel the steering wheel start to shake. I'd usually top out at about 90 mph for long rides like this.

I don't remember much of my accident that night. One minute I was getting into my car, and the next I was lying on my back on the highway looking skyward. There were bright flashing lights, the squawking of walkie-talkie chatter, and the sickening smell of gasoline. My vision was blurry, but I could see that my car was upside down and firemen were throwing some kind of powder on the ground around it. The German police placed me under arrest for DWI, and took me to the *Krankenhaus*--their word for hospital--for evaluation.

U.S. Military Police were supposed to take me back to my base from this hospital--presumably to the brig. But since I had alcohol poisoning, I needed to stay here a couple of days until I was stabilized. (I had no real physical injuries other than cuts and bruises.) Later, I was told that the German police wanted to keep me in their custody and prosecute me, but had relented at the urging of my base commander. I remember thinking: *"Where the fuck am I, and what's gonna happen now? Shit....."*

Lying there in that hospital while handcuffed and under guard, I had a lot of time to think. I was remembering the many hell-raising episodes that had led up to this quagmire. In the months before I flipped my car, I was always out carousing.

For instance, one night at a club, some French Canadian soldiers started a big fistfight and I got stabbed in the back of the neck with a broken wine glass. At the base hospital, since it was late, the only person available to treat me was a young medic, right out of training. He didn't ask any questions beyond "What happened?" He just directed me into an operating room, told me lie down on my stomach, and nervously focused this huge light down onto my bloody neck. I remember trying to calm him by laughing it off, saying, "Yeah, we kicked their asses." It took him a full hour to put in ten stitches because his hands kept shaking, and I talked him through it by repeating, "OK, good, you got it; it doesn't hurt, great." The next morning at work, some of the Cadre were all abuzz about the big bandage that was on my neck, and the Commandant called me in to reprimand me. At lunchtime that same day, I drove to the nearby Ramstein Air Force Base mall and bought a set of weights and a lifting bench. Later at dinner, one soldier ran up to me, laughing, and said, "Hey Jerry, all of those fuckin' older guys saw you lugging those weights into your building and started moaning to each other: 'Oh no, now he's only gonna be stronger!'"

So, now it was the third day after the car accident, and two American MPs had finally shown up to sign me out of the German hospital and transport me to a nearby US Army base. When we got there, they ordered me into a chilly holding cell. I was told that I'd stay there overnight, then I'd be transferred back to my own base to face the Commandant again. I figured I was looking at a Court Martial, or an Article 15 at the very least.

"Excuse me, Sergeant. Can I just use the bathroom over there?" I pleaded with the MP who was sitting behind the desk reading a newspaper.

"Use the toilet that's right back there in the corner of the cell," he replied.

"No look, there's toilet paper jammed in there; it's all messed up. Just let me use that one, please!" I pointed toward a bathroom door that I saw out near the MP station.

On the ride over, I'd conversed with both of the MPs in a free-flowing, friendly way. They didn't seem to be hard-ass, strict types; they were just doing their job.

He replied, "I don't know. Wait a minute; let me see." With that, he left the room. He came back in with the other MP that had driven with us. They both looked through the bars at the backed-up toilet in the corner, and the one that had just come in nodded and said, "OK, hurry up."

All I could think about on the ride over was, "How am I gonna get out of this?" This was serious. I worried: *What if I get a dishonorable discharge? I'd be a failure. I'd have to go back to Brooklyn.*

Then, I had a brainstorm. My plan was simple. *I'll make believe that I'm totally distraught--and fake trying to kill myself, right here in front of them. Then the Army will let me off easy. I'm a good soldier otherwise…. Yeah, this is a great idea.*

The MP unlocked the cell door and swung it open. Both MP's watched me carefully as I made my way about 15 feet down the hallway toward the bathroom. I was smiling appreciatively, nodding my head, and saying, "Thanks, thank you; I'll only be a minute."

Once I was inside the bathroom, I felt my heart beating heavily. I was suddenly bright-eyed and alert; I was on a high-priority mission.

My eyes scanned the ceiling and window areas, looking for something to tie my belt to. Seeing the plumbing pipes running close, but not flush against the wall behind the toilet tank, and up high, was more than I could ask for. Perfect! I closed down the toilet seat lid and stepped up so that I could stand on the seat. After quickly sliding off my belt, I looped it around one of the rusty, paint-chipped pipes. I noticed that it shook a bit as I started to tie a knot and thought, "Fuck, I hope it doesn't collapse when I jump." I forced the thought from my mind.

With my belt tightly tied to the pipe, I now started wrapping the other end around my neck. *Shit, it was too short!* It wouldn't make it around my neck and still leave me enough length to tie a knot. I told myself: *"Hurry up, think!"* Looking down, I saw that if I stepped up higher, and onto the toilet's water tank, I'd probably have enough slack in the belt to make it work. I couldn't get up there though, without grabbing onto one of the overhead pipes for balance. After I'd placed one foot up on top of the tank and then the other, I thought, "Man, this is really high up!" I finished wrapping the belt around my neck and knotted it. Then, I placed both of my hands, with my palms facing my chest, near where my neck met the belt. Now, I curled all of my fingers except my thumbs toward me and jammed them down snugly into the space between my neck and the belt. I waited. About five minutes had passed since I'd begun fussing with the belt.

I stood completely still, precariously perched on top of the toilet tank and wondered how long it would be before they came looking. More minutes passed. I kept thinking: *"Where are they?"* Fatigue was setting in and it was getting harder to balance myself. I'd jump as soon as I heard someone open the door, and my fingers, wrapped so tightly around the noose, would allow me to use my upper-body strength and suspend myself in the air. I was sure I'd be able to do this; I had the strength. I'd become very proficient at chin-ups after suffering great humiliation in front of my sixth-grade gym class when I couldn't do even one of them.

"Hey, you done?" The sound of the MP's voice was muffled from behind the door. He knocked hard on the door. "You OK? Hurry up!"

Standing frozen like a statue, I didn't answer. Complete silence. I'd purposely left the door unlocked. I knew it would open any second. I heard him yell again, now louder: "Hey, what are you doing?" I didn't make a peep. Just then the door opened. I jumped.

"Gurgle, gurgle, fuuh, ssshh." I was kicking my legs around, flailing violently, making all of these horrible choking noises while simultaneously spitting and drooling for good measure. Man, was I good; what an actor! I was holding my entire weight up by just eight little fingers, which now were being severely crushed by the belt, and were hurting terribly--much more than I had anticipated.

"Help, help, get help!" The MP who opened the door started shouting back over his shoulder as he rushed to administer a bear hug around my lower legs. I immediately started to panic because now I couldn't save myself should my fingers slip out accidentally. His tight grip around my legs would prevent me from being able to maneuver my feet back onto the top of the toilet tank. I couldn't believe this! Holy Shit! I was wriggling around like a fuckin' vertical earthworm trying to escape capture.

Several soldiers burst into the bathroom in an explosion of frenetic energy! They were all trying to hold me up, but kept yelling, "Get him down, get him down!" At this point I'm thinking, "THANK FUCKIN' GOD! Get me the fuck out of here, please!" I think I pissed my pants.

The German Nuthouse and the Frog

"Hello, my name is Dr. Ramos. How are you feeling?"

Almost nine hours had passed from the time that I was "rescued" at the MP station and then transferred to the psychiatric ward of the base hospital. It was three in the morning and I hadn't slept since the previous night. Physically and mentally exhausted, I desperately needed to lie down and rest.

"Uh, look, I'm OK," I replied. "Can I just please get a bed and go to sleep?"

Dr. Ramos was sitting up perfectly straight, directly in front of me, about five feet away. He had one leg politely crossed over the other, was holding a yellow legal pad and a pen, and spoke very softly while giving me this creepy smile. The strange vibe that I felt was only amplified by the surroundings--a stark white room with nothing on the walls and no furniture, and just the two metal folding chairs in which we were sitting. Trying to make an improvised cot out of the uncomfortable chair, I slid down low and extended my legs way out in front of me.

I continued, "I know what you're thinking. They told you that I tried to hang myself. Believe me, I didn't really want to die: I was just pretending. I was trying to get out of trouble for my DWI and car crash--I swear!"

This nerdy-looking doctor went on calmly smiling at me, and occasionally looked down to scribble on his pad while I rambled on. He was clearly not convinced.

He pressed: "How did you get that scar on your face, and the ones on your chest?"

Because I had a V-neck shirt on, he could see that I had a long, raised five-inch scar running up on an angle across my chest. There were several other scars of varying length below that one, too. Back when I was 15, some older men of foreign descent, who lived in a rundown apartment building in the neighborhood, had come out waving sticks and complaining that they didn't want us kids across the street hanging out and selling drugs. All of the other kids ran away, and I was left to be beaten up by them. I raced the two blocks home, crying and yelling along the way that I would get them back. No one was home, and I rushed into my bedroom to retrieve a box cutter. In a mad frenzy, I took off my shirt, extended the razor blade out from the housing, exposing the cutting edge, positioned it on the upper right side of my chest, and started ripping across the skin. I kept yelling out loud, "I'll fuckin' kill you all, you're all dead," while slashing myself again and again, and again.

Why had I turned into some sort of a wild Indian ritualistically preparing for battle? Because I was really afraid of those men who'd beat me up, but I didn't want to allow them to get away with what they'd done. I ran back to the building full of blood, continuing to yell out loud to no one in particular, and then I started throwing garbage cans and bottles at their windows. I unscrewed the big, heavy metal caps off of a fire hydrant sent them crashing though the plate glass windows on the front doors. This time, no one came out to confront me. Police were called, and I was brought back home to my mom who was just coming in. The two officers were in shock and dismay after they questioned me and came to understand that I had mutilated myself. My scars are still hard to explain when someone sees them and shrieks, "What happened?"

As Dr. Ramos waited patiently for my reply to his question, I could tell that my explanation about getting the scars in a fight did not satisfy him. Skepticism was etched into his face.

I begged, "Please doctor, look, look right into my eyes. See? You can see that that I'm not crazy, right?" My tone was desperate.

Of course the question I posed only convinced him that we'd need to talk several more hours! He'd finish his evaluation when he felt I was not in immediate danger of hurting myself.

~

"Eh, eh, I'm da Frog; eh, eh. Eh, eh, I'm da Frog; yeah, the Frog; eh, eh. That's right, the Frog; eh, eh...."

You know when you're sleeping and you hear something and wake up, but you don't open your eyes right away because you're so exhausted, you just listen? By the time Dr. Ramos had finally let me go to sleep, it was almost time for me to get up.

What is that? Who is that? Then I remembered: *Oh man, I'm in bed at the psychiatric ward!* With my eyes still closed, I could hear mumbling, the rustling of papers, things being moved about... and most disturbing of all, I could hear The Frog.

"Eh, eh, I'm da Frog; eh, eh...."

Rolling over and opening my eyes, I saw this little unshaven guy standing there. He had jet-black greasy hair. His hands were stuffed down tightly into his hospital robe pockets. And he kept saying, "Eh, eh, I'm da Frog...."

My plan had backfired. Now I'd be in the looney bin. But for how long?

Returning to the Danger Zone

When I was finally released back to my unit after three weeks of medication, group therapy, and actually getting to know "The Frog" and of all his hopes and dreams, I was summoned yet again to the Commandant's office.

Because I was a productive soldier when I wasn't under the influence, the punishment meted out to me that time was minor—all I got was another base restriction, an assignment to mow grass every night, and some stern words. Nevertheless, I repeatedly relapsed. I kept getting in more trouble, and found myself back in front of the Commandant, again and again. Finally, he realized he'd had enough of me. He simply said: "Castaldo, you are out of control. You're going home! OK? We'll call you if there's a war."

Depressive doubt filled my mind. I started to wonder if I could ever truly stay sober, off drugs, and get back to "who I was originally." I mean, my grandfather had been a severe alcoholic. He even drank rubbing alcohol. Eventually, he fell down a flight of stairs and died. My dad was a heavy drinker for a very long time, too, although he managed to quit on his own later in life. I wondered: *Isn't it hereditary? Will that be me?*

The following week I found myself standing in front of a Judicial Army Review Board while I strenuously pleaded my case. "Please don't send me home." I begged, but to no avail. The clerk read out loud: "Private Jerry Castaldo, please rise. You are hereby separated from the United States Army with a General Discharge for failing to maintain standards for retention."

During my flight out of Germany with a destination of Fort Dix, N.J. for out-processing, I wondered what I'd encounter back in the neighborhood. My new plan was to find work immediately. I resolved to straighten out my life. Again.

On my way into my mom's apartment building, I managed to bypass the locked vestibule door without having to use the intercom by piggy-backing in with another neighbor. I got upstairs, knocked, and hoped that my mother would not be too shocked by my being back home so much sooner than she had expected.

I heard the peephole cover slide back and forth, the door opened, and I mumbled awkwardly, "Hi, Ma."

Jerry Castaldo

Thrust Back to the Neighborhood

Winter 1981--Age 22

#1 Song of the radio: "Starting Over"—John Lennon

Hope is my favorite word. It's all encompassing and it's the one that I always held onto despite my multitude of failures; there was still hope for me.

The Army had saved my life by getting me off the streets and out of the country. It had built confidence in me and I knew I'd miss it. It was like being in a gang again, but a good gang. There was a sense of belonging and of feeling patriotic. I was housed, fed and protected. But now I was back in New York sooner than I had planned and it was time to take action, positive action. Within one short week of my being home, I'd landed a job on Wall Street, in the back office of a noted brokerage firm. As a teen I had been a messenger on Wall Street, and so now I decided that the fantasy of getting into show business was over. It was time to enter the work force and fall in line with everyone else. I'd work my way up to becoming a stock broker.

Within a couple of months I'd approached my supervisor about the firm paying for me to attend the New York Institute of Finance to take courses. I'd also applied to Pace University for additional schooling. Because I'd dropped out of Brooklyn Technical High School during my freshman year, though, Pace wouldn't accept me without my having earned additional credits; so I ditched that idea. I started at the Institute of Finance and began my ambitious climb to the top.

"Where is Jerry going now? Look, he always just gets up and leaves. To where, for what? I don't know, do you?" This is what my other lowly colleagues were asking each other every day. Any time they'd question me directly, I'd reply that I had a "meeting."

Since I was now going to be an executive, I was going to start acting like one. I had carefully observed how the upper-echelon department-heads were dressed and adjusted accordingly. I purchased those ugly black wing-tip shoes, bright white button-down Oxford shirts, and suits in solid colors of navy-blue and gray. My ridiculously expensive black leather briefcase resembled the kind doctors used to carry back in the old days. I'd rise at 4:45 am, run a few miles along the darkened streets of Brooklyn, shower with the always-just-lukewarm water in our perpetually chilly apartment, and get to the huge clerks' desk at Donaldson, Lufkin & Jenrette at 7:45 am sharp--on time, every morning. The eight of us at that desk, all in our early 20's, would sit there all day tearing giant dot-matrix printer sheets to do visual checks and comparisons, while marking them with a pen--very boring and tedious. There were a total of about 50 other people in this huge room that housed the P & S department.

"Jerry, come here; I want to talk to you...." Now it was my supervisor wanting to ask where I'd been disappearing to every day at different intervals. I explained to him that the higher-ups were grooming me for another position across the street at Pershing and Company, the firm with which we'd recently merged. I went on to tell him that if he had a problem, he should talk to Ralph Castaldo. Ralph was the vice president in charge of the entire floor, and everyone was afraid to talk to him; he was so strict and aloof. Responding to my supervisor's questioning, I was implying nepotism— although in truth, I wasn't even related to Ralph Castaldo. My supervisor never called my bluff by going to talk to Ralph--and he never questioned me about my absences again.

So, several times a day, I continued to don my suit jacket, pick up my briefcase (filled with nothing of real importance), and head across the street. I'd visit different brokers who worked on the trading desk and told them I was assigned to sit in and learn the ropes. This charade went on undetected for months, and I actually did learn and make some valuable connections. It culminated in my being invited to an expensive dinner party at the exclusive Wall Street restaurant, "Harry's at Hanover," which was closed off to all but some top people at the firm. I'll never forget the expression on Ralph Castaldo's face when he looked across the huge dinner table and, with great surprise, saw one of his clerks toasting a drink with one of the firm's top regional directors. Over the din of busy conversation, I smiled at him and loudly asked, "Hi Ralph! Fabulous party isn't it?"

Eventually, though, the reality of how the business world really works unfolded. Ivy League students who were on their summer break and referred to as "Summer Associates" were the ones really being wooed and groomed for placement. My act was by now foiled, and I was once again sitting at the clerks' desk mired in monotony. I'd occasionally find refuge by taking a copy of the *New York Post* into the men's room and daydream about show business again. The firm had told me that they were not going to sponsor me for my Registered Rep test to become a broker because of my lack of college credits. Even though I argued that selling stocks doesn't require formal education, they passed on me. Now, in the smelly, marble toilet stall, I was reading about French playboy Philippe Junot and his wife, Princess Caroline of Monaco, and other such glamorous stories about the well-heeled. I also started reading reviews of singers appearing in Manhattan clubs, written by Curt Davis (who was then the cabaret critic for the *New York Post)*. One day while sitting there, pants down around my ankles, I closed the newspaper and thought to myself, "Goodbye Wall Street."

Testing the Showbiz Waters

"Lemme have a *Village Voice,"* I barked over the squeal of the subway trains grinding the curving steel tracks into the station. The newsstand at the 14th Street Station in Manhattan was right under Union Square Park--a popular place to score drugs back then before it was cleaned up in the '90s by the Giuliani administration. Seven years later, I would find myself lying down there on those very tracks, severely injured and unconscious.

Since I would now pursue show business full time, I figured I'd have to buy the *Village Voice*—as soon as it was delivered to newsstands every Wednesday--and also *Back Stage* (the showbiz weekly)--every Thursday—just to stay on top of auditions happening around the city. In the meantime, I'd work at temporary jobs. I was, for a while, a security-guard at the Metropolitan Club; I worked for Eastern Onion Singing Telegrams; I answered telephones; I worked at Shanghai Bank in the World Trade Center--anything I could get. My Army health-benefits were intact since I hadn't been dishonorably discharged, and I was sure happy for that. Living again with my mom and brother in Brooklyn, I had to sneak off to Manhattan each day to avoid the old crew who now knew that I was home again. God forbid they'd find out I was pursuing the arts, lest I be called "a fuckin' fag."

~

"Hello? Hi, my name is Jerry and I'm answering your ad in *The Voice* for a guitar player who sings. Is this Anne?"

Anne Rebold was teaching high school in Brooklyn and was also a talented pianist who would perform wherever she could. She'd placed an ad and I called her. She didn't live too far away. So it was easy to rehearse and then to start doing shows around the city with her. My idea was to switch musical genres so that I could actually work in the long-term as a singer. I'd always played rock music in local bands. But I figured that if I switched to the "Great American Songbook," I could get into the Manhattan clubs and maybe eventually get reviewed, and start a career.

Anne and I worked out an act and started auditioning. We did some restaurant shows and even did a New

Year's Eve performance at a mob-run clam house in Bensonhurst. Things got exciting when we got into Pips Comedy Club in Sheepshead Bay. This is where comedian David Brenner had gotten his start under the tutelage of the club's owner, George Schultz. Brenner then went on to a great success and would even host "The Tonight Show" when Johnny Carson would take a night off. George had two sons who were running the place, and one of them, Seth Schultz, would bring me in to perform, paying me just $10.00 to cover carfare. I didn't care about the low pay, though; we had an audience and we were hanging around people like comic Andrew Silverstein--who'd eventually create the stage name Andrew "Dice" Clay. Some years down the road, when I met Jerry Seinfeld, I found out that Anne and I had just missed him by a couple of years—since he'd started out at Pips, too. He'd used the club as a springboard to get to the "Catch a Rising Star" club in Manhattan and late-night television talk shows.

~

"I'm sorry; I don't speak *Qualudian*," Andrew "Dice" Clay snarled sarcastically at Stevie Bones; the club erupted into laughter.

After people in the neighborhood heard I was singing at Pips, they'd gotten together in a group to come see me. Of course Stevie Bones was curious to see what I was doing--and as usual, he was sloshed. So when Andrew "Dice" Clay caught him talking loudly to someone else in the audience during his set, he focused in on Stevie and tried to start a dialogue with him. But Andrew couldn't understand a word Stevie was saying.... The audience found Andrew's "Qualudian" ad lib hilarious.

Stevie was not so amused. He simply said, "Fuck that guy," and made a retreat to the club's bathroom.

I enjoyed being part of nights like this. Especially since everyone from the neighborhood was there seeing me having some success.

Not too far from Pips, there was a "hot sheets" hotel called The Golden Gate Inn and I had heard they hosted a weekly talent contest. (I also heard that the Golden Gate Inn was a main meeting place for gangster Sammy "The Bull" Gravano and his cohorts.) Anne and I entered the contest and I sang Bobby Darin's hit, "Mack the Knife." I remember kicking my leg up awkwardly in the middle of it, and drunken patrons at the bar bursting into applause. And to my surprise, Anne and I won! They handed me a small white envelope containing 25 dollars. This was great. I remember staring down at the writing in black Magic Marker ink that said "First Prize," and thinking to myself, as I walked to the men's room: *"I'm on my way...."*

"Holy shit! I can't believe it! What are you doing here? Were you out there at the bar? Did you see me sing?" I asked.

Standing at the grimy men's-room sink as we locked eyes was "Crazy Sal." The last time I'd heard about him, I was in Germany looking at his photo in the newspaper after he'd been arrested for murder.

"Jerry, Jerry Castaldo. How are ya? Whataya--you a singer now? Ha, ha! Yeah, I wasn't sure at first if that was you out there. That was pretty good, fucko," said Sal, as he extended his hand to shake mine.

I searched for a way to pose the question gently. But then instead just blurted out nervously what I was wondering: "I thought you were in jail, Sal?" He explained to me that he'd been out on bail; in fact, the very next morning was the start of his trial. After ten minutes of small-talk, we shook hands again and parted. That was the last time I ever saw him.

~

"Hey you black bastard, I told you to give me that bar of soap! It's right there. See it? On the sink, there. Get if for me!" I yelled. "I asked you nicely--but you wanna be a prick, right?"

The police officer assigned to sit at my bedside here in Coney Island Hospital had gone to use the bathroom. As I lay here--handcuffed to the bed and under arrest in this second-floor room—I had an idea. If I could get that bar of soap and spit on it to work up a slippery lather, maybe I'd be able to slip off the handcuffs, jump out of the second-floor window, and escape out into the snowy street. I was wearing only a flimsy hospital gown.

After the cop who was guarding me came back into the room, the black man that I'd tried enlisting to help me with my plot complained to the cop about me. The only reason I was trying to execute that stupid plan was because I was still high. I might add that some of my best friends in the Army were black; hell, I'd even dated some black girls. So no, I'm not a racist; yet, I sure sounded like one that particular day. What was I doing in a hospital? I had time to think about that.

Anne and I had done a show somewhere, and then gotten some liquor and food before retiring to her apartment. And, yes, I was drinking again. After she had fallen asleep, I'd taken her car keys during the middle of the night and had driven to Carnegie Hall, on 57th Street in Manhattan. I knew that Frank Sinatra was appearing there that night. After I'd arrived, I just sat there, staring at Sinatra's poster displayed in the glass case on the wall. A cassette tape of him singing was playing in the car. (This wasn't the first time I'd engaged in this kind of strange inspirational ceremony. After I'd read Sinatra's biography some months before this, I'd jumped on a Path train to his birthplace of Hoboken, NJ to see the house he grew up in. I stood in front of it and had kept inching backward, further and further into the street, so that I could get a better view. At that point, my heel slid into something mushy. When I looked down and saw that I was standing in a huge pile of fresh, stinking dog shit, I was so happy and smiled! I remembered hearing that it's good luck when that happens.)

I sat in the car, in front of Carnegie Hall early that morning, listening to the tape of Sinatra singing, and I drank.... Driving home, on the Brooklyn Queens

Expressway, I wound up crashing Anne's car. I was amazed at the damage to it. Somehow, the floor on the driver's side was ripped open so you could actually see the street below. My foot was badly injured, too. Still, I hopped out of the car, hobbled away from the scene and off the highway before cops arrived.

As I made my way down a street in the Red Hook section of Brooklyn, I noticed that someone had left their car running to warm it up. (It was freezing that morning.) I proceeded to steal the car--and wound up crashing that one, too. This time I was promptly arrested. After that, I might add, Anne ignored all of my phone calls. I'd never see or hear from her ever again.

The Brooklyn Criminal Court judge offered me thirty days in rehab in exchange for no jail time and no probation. I took it, happy to have that break—even if it meant placement in a locked ward--no visitors or calls allowed. The only contact that I'd have with the outside world was by mail.

After it was all over, I remember waiting on line for the rehab clerks to finish up my paperwork so that I could get out. "OK, Castaldo, you're discharged; we don't want to see you back here," a nurse told me, with a stern look in her eyes.

Unfortunately, I didn't take the suggestion she offered that I should follow up by participating in AA. For that, I would suffer dire consequences.

The Start of a Real Performing Career

Giro Castaldo. That's my real name, the one on my birth certificate. I was wondering if that name was too ethnic for show business. In the old days, would-be entertainers would change their name to avoid stereotyping and typecasting, but did I need to do it now in the 1980's?

Through sheer will and determination, I refrained from drinking and drugging for many months as I ventured daily into Manhattan for auditions. This is known as "white knuckling it" among addicts who are in recovery. Their theory is that "will power" alone—which I was relying on--will not keep you sober, and you can only stay sober by being part of the "community" of others like yourself. To that I said, "Bullshit!"

I landed parts in a few non-union plays, did some student films for NYU and the University of Bridgeport, and was cast in a few local commercials. One play I had a major role in that was technically off-off Bway, ran in the Theatre District in Times Square for three months, and we even won a rave review in the *New York Times.* I parlayed this notice into getting myself booked onto the legendary "Joe Franklin Show" on TV. My panel-mate was actor Fisher Stevens, who later went on to win an Academy Award. I pushed hard and was able to get my photo into the *Daily News* and the *New York Post* too. This boosted my confidence.

"Thank you, NEXT!" Screamed the bespeckled woman seated at the long table with four other grim-looking people who were conducting the audition.

This was getting tough. After I'd started talking my way into bigger, more important auditions for musical theatre, my lack of training showed, and I was promptly rejected over and over again. This was reminding me a bit of Wall Street. People who had graduated from Julliard, the Yale School of Drama, and other such recognized institutions were whisked in to audition, coddled, and treated much differently. I'd never had any voice training, and my self-taught rendition of the song "Maria" from *West Side Story* was laughable. My horrible rendition of "Yes, We Have No Bananas" would also make auditors' eyes' roll.

In addition, you were often required to dance before you were allowed to sing at these musical-theatre auditions, so I'd never even make it through the first phase. To remedy this problem, I applied for a grant at NYU to attend classes with the American Dance Machine, a well-respected dance troupe based on the Upper East Side. The harsh reality, however, was that my classmates were already trained dancers from a very young age, and the sessions moved so quickly that I couldn't follow anything. What a pitiful sight I was, proudly dressed in my shiny new black tights and spandex tank top, wearing white Capezio jazz shoes, stiffly arabesque-ing about the studio like some spastic person with advanced motor skill problems. What an idiot I felt like. So I quit. *so funny!*

Because of the advanced level of physical training that I'd been able to attain while in the Army, I was motivated to keep up my exercise schedule and started to immerse myself in books on the subject. Subsequently, this helped me find work in various health clubs around the city. After I completed some additional training, I was able to teach aerobic dance, calisthenics, and yoga. I continued to audition for anything and I was able to weasel my way into several big-budget films as an extra. Rubbing elbows with some major Hollywood heavyweights helped me regain confidence, and made me want to work hard and stay sober. But no matter how much I wanted that, I just couldn't do it.

"Holy shit, man! Look! The cop is smoking pot, ha, ha!" The teenager sitting on the stoop of the small apartment building was enjoying the sight of my having one of the other kids light my joint for me.

This particular film that I was working on had me dressed in a New York City police uniform and driving a police car in an action scene. It was an all-night shoot in Manhattan's Chinatown. Actors Matt Dillon and Daniel Stern were on the set and very friendly. Sadly, though, I was back to my old ways again; I had dropped a tab of acid at the start of this shoot because I thought it would be fun to work on the film while tripping.

During a break, I walked around the corner and off the set--still wearing my cop uniform--to smoke a joint. These kids gave me a light.

For them, it was a visually funny moment. But for me, it was just another sign of the tragedy that would later come.

NYC Politician Andrew J. Stein Adopts Me

Winter 1983--Age 24

#1 song on the radio: Michael Jackson—"Billie Jean"

"Hey, Jerry--there's some lady on the phone who's looking for a private trainer. Come over here, you should take this," the young female receptionist whispered excitedly to me, while covering the mouthpiece of the phone with her hand.

"Excuse me, sir, let me just get rid of this call; I'll be back in a minute," I politely assured the older man with whom I was working. He looked relieved to take a break from his exercising, and nodded his sweating head obligingly as he plopped down into a nearby chair.

By now I'd worked at several different health clubs in Manhattan and was training people one-on-one, both at the gym and in their homes. I also had a huge following of people who took my daily aerobics classes up to seven times a week. Sometimes I'd have a hundred people dancing in sync with my beat-driven, loud music. We had a huge room with walls mirrored all the way up to the ceiling—and the ceiling was mirrored, too. Club members would line up early outside the door for a chance to get into my class, which was known for being tough, but not too "dancey"--as I knew that would discourage less coordinated people from trying it. I went to great lengths to keep people motivated by making superior "mix tapes" that I'd use in class. Wow! Really

More than once there was pushing and shoving, and once even a fistfight erupted as devotees tried not to get

123

shut out of my swelling classes. Helping people lose weight and also guiding them through the confusing maze of fitness equipment made me feel useful. I'm also convinced that addressing these large groups of people on a daily basis for several years helped me develop an ease with verbal patter for when I was really "on stage."

I took the phone from the receptionist and listened carefully. The woman would only tell me that she needed a trainer for her husband; she wouldn't give me any more information. After quoting a price to her, she agreed with it and I figured I'd just make the first meeting exploratory and assess her husband's fitness-level then. She gave me an address, a phone number for me to call should there be a problem-- and a six am appointment for me to arrive on the Upper East Side.

It was an encouraging time for me; I was very happy to now be living with my girlfriend Mary Lou, and not drinking or taking any kind of hard drugs. I was really trying--although smoking marijuana was something that I was not willing to give up back then, so for about two years you might say I was "mostly" sober. I mean, pot never made my life unmanageable, although of course it's terrible for your lungs and your health in general. I was a popular fitness-instructor who really cared about improving peoples' lives--while simultaneously fighting my own problem with addiction and trying to get a foothold in show business.

This job turned out to be fun because I'd also wind up working with some celebrities, including Carly Simon and Bill Cosby. The military had taught me how to push myself physically, and I liked helping others do the same. My main concern was getting people to challenge themselves so that they could reach new levels of fitness and achieve weight goals, but I was fanatical about stressing safety first. From what I could see during the health-club boom of the '80s, under qualified and under-trained personnel were sometimes actually hurting people. There were no regulations back then; you didn't need any certification to call yourself a trainer. Health clubs could save money by not hiring people with degrees in exercise physiology. Of course, I was one of those without formal education and training-- but I was so into doing the right job that I read voraciously on the subject.

~

"Oh wow, what a nice surprise...." I probably couldn't have uttered a more appropriate phrase to endear myself to then-Manhattan-Borough-President Andrew J. Stein. I'd left Brooklyn at 4:00 am, and had taken a bus and two trains to arrive here at this luxury apartment building on time. Since I would read all three of the major daily New York newspapers every day anyway, I never minded the long, slow, chugging subway ride from the far reaches of Brooklyn into upper Manhattan. For me, the traveling was "research time" to study showbiz-related articles.

"Hi, how are you," Stein said to me, expressing his reply as more of a statement than a question. "Come in," he instructed. As I stepped into this big, beautiful apartment—which, given my background, felt quite foreign to me--I quickly tried to remember exactly where I'd seen him before and who he was. From my voluminous reading, I suddenly remembered that he was a politician and his exact name came to me, right down to the middle initial.

Then I remembered more about him. Stein had been instrumental, some years back before that time, in exposing and bringing to justice the villainous Bernard Bergman, a terrible nursing-home czar who'd allowed elder-abuse in his facilities. Subsequently, because of Stein's involvement in this investigation, Bergman was jailed, and New York State implemented new laws regarding long-term care facilities. It made big news at the time, and it certainly was a feather in his cap. I remembered, too, that Stein's father, Jerry Finklestein, was a multi-millionaire who published the *New York Law Journal* and was friends with such notables as Nelson Rockefeller and Hubert Humphrey. And now, here I was--helping Andrew Stein to work out!

After I left his place that first morning, I started to digest the dialogue that we'd had. For starters, he'd told me he wanted to work out four times a week at this same early hour! My shift at the New York Health & Racquet Club, across the street from St. Patrick's Cathedral, didn't start until well after noon and would last until eight pm. So I'd be putting in very long hours. The schedule would be tough, but I agreed. The "dead time" I'd have each morning, between working for him and working for the Racquet Club, would be good for auditions, I reasoned. Plus, I really liked him. Despite the fact that he was fourteen years older than me and from a totally different world, we had an instant rapport.

~

"What's my name? Jerry, tell me--what's my name?" Andrew Stein yelled with a maniacal face, eyes darting left and right, turning his head side-to-side, while blowing deep breaths out forcefully!

"Ferrigno," I shouted. "You are FER-IGGG-NOOO. Push, push; come on, FERRIGNO, get tough. PUSH!"

This was what you'd hear in the gym room of Stein's apartment when we'd be in session. He had met--and was friends with--many celebrities, but he always seemed to be really excited by the males who were able to achieve "mass." Muscle mass. I remember he went on a vitamin buying-spree after he'd had dinner with Arnold Schwarzenegger, up at the Kennedy Compound in Hyannis Port, Massachusetts. I disagreed with him over the wisdom of his spending hundreds of dollars a month on vitamins; my research had led me to believe in a balanced diet and any kind of multivitamin--period. For women, just make sure it's a multivitamin with Iron--and then they were covered, too. But I guess he found fitness advice coming from Schwarzenegger sound.

"I'm Ferrigno, right? Jerry. WHO AM I?" Stein shouted at me, white foamy spittle spraying onto his lower lip.

"Yes, yes, you are--Ferr-iggg-nooo. YOU'RE AN ANIMAL. PUSH!" I yelled back at him intensely.

Lou Ferrigno was the actor who played the "Incredible Hulk" on TV. He'd grown up in Brooklyn, and had gone to the same high school that I had briefly attended (although he was several years ahead of me)--Brooklyn Technical. Lou's brother Andy and their dad, a retired Police Lieutenant, sold gym equipment on McDonald Avenue, back in the neighborhood.

After realizing that we'd need additional equipment if Andrew Stein really did want to turn himself into "The Hulk," I went to see the Ferrignos and made a substantial purchase from them. Now, with actual weight plates that said "Ferrigno" on them, he was even more psyched than ever about working out. I must say, he did work very hard; I was very impressed with his drive and dedication in improving his general health.

This man helped me in many ways during that first year; I was greatly appreciative. He gave me multiple pay raises without my asking for them; he recommended me to other potential clients with Fifth Avenue addresses; and he even allowed me to use his name as a reference on job applications. All of this help enabled me to afford a very nice large one-bedroom apartment in Manhattan, and that made my early-morning commute to him easier. Despite all of this good fortune that I was having, though, I remember feeling slightly depressed; it was a bit difficult to see how the wealthy lived compared to my family. It had an odd, startling effect on me.

Plucked from Street Singing and Off To Florida

A couple of times in my late teens I'd experimented with singing on the street in Manhattan for passersby. My new plan now was to sing every day in public, for hours at a time, and see what might happen. This would be intense on-the-job training in honing my then-minimal skills in attracting and entertaining a diverse audience.

I set up shop on the sidewalk directly across the street from Radio City Music Hall, complete with two portable rechargeable amplifiers, a microphone, a Sony walkman to play back taped backing-tracks, and a sign that said, "The Jerry Castaldo Show." The small luggage-cart that I had modified was perfect for transporting everything around. I'd store the equipment in a locked closet at the health club in which I worked, and then I'd roll it up the street to Sixth Avenue for my performances. I figured this had to be a pretty safe spot in which to do my shows. Previously, I had tried performing up in Times Square, but that hadn't worked out. Late one weekend night, a gang of black kids who couldn't have been more than fourteen years old had swarmed in on me and stolen all of the money from my open guitar case. Then they'd scattered out in all directions like bugs. So now I was giving a new neighborhood a try.

"Jer-ry, Jer-ry, Jer-ry...." I'd heard this chant before; I smiled back and waved. After a few months of street shows, many lunch-time office-workers in the area knew my name and would yell it out and stop by to say hi. Even the street vendors working their various carts all knew me and would offer me free hot dogs and pretzels. The most surprising thing to me was that after I'd scoop up the money from my case each day, I'd have an average of between $100.00 and $150.00 dollars for only three or four hours' work. I was making more money singing out there than I was making at the health club!

One day, when I was out singing on the street, a tall good-looking woman, who was about 30, dropped her business card into my open case along with a ten-dollar bill. She didn't say a word. She just smiled at me and walked on. This mysterious woman would later radically change my life.

In the same period of time, the cosmetics giant Revlon Inc. was mounting an ambitious trade show that was to tour 25 cities around the United States. They advertised in *Back Stage* that they were looking for a Master of Ceremonies who could sing and do a little clean comedy.

After several intense auditions and interviews with the corporate brass, I was hired to host these Revlon shows. I remember flying to Boston with a group of executives for the first performance, and thinking: *Even though the money I'm getting for this is good, I'm not going to stop doing my street shows.* I was convinced that singing on the street was good exposure--and having the occasional big-name celebrity stop by to pat me on the back was a thrill, too.

The Revlon shows were going rather well, I thought; it felt good to be part of this colorful extravaganza. Then one day the show's director left me an urgent message to call him back. The tone of his voice on the phone message was enough to get me worrying. When I called back, I got the devastating news that the tour was being cancelled.

Having the support of my girlfriend, Mary Lou, was very valuable to me at this time. But the seams of our relationship were beginning to show signs of wear. We'd been together for about ten years and although we really loved each other, as I've pointed out before, there were times that we both strayed. Most would agree that this is normal and healthy behavior for teenagers and young adults—you want to see who else might be out there. We'd eventually always wind up back together again.

Sadly, though, I was starting to feel more like "brother and sister" with her by now; the aura of sexual excitement had waned. I wasn't specifically looking for a new romance, but the ongoing, nagging thought that I had was, "Am I really ready to spend the rest of my life with her?" Only later, after she and I had endured a nightmarish event that tore us apart abruptly and forever, did I realize that she'd certainly set the bar high for others who would come after her. Inevitably and unfairly, I'd compare any new love-interest I'd have with her almost saint-like, altruistic ways. Each new woman I met had to compete with what I can only describe as Mary Lou's incredible "goodness factor."

~

"Where is that business card?" I struggled to remember. The bombshell of my being informed that the

Revlon tour was not going to continue propelled me into action. I would call that woman who'd left her card during my street show. I remembered it said, "Manager of *The Yacht High Spirits.*" After finding the card and calling the number that was ostentatiously embossed on it in gold, I was connected to Shelly Malone. We talked for almost an hour. She invited me to fly down to Florida to sing on the yacht for the dinner parties that she regularly booked for business execs and their clients. Within a few days, I had hand-picked a reliable trainer from my health club to work with Andrew Stein during my absence; I packed my bags and headed south.

Besides traveling with the Army, I never really had been anywhere else completely on my own. Landing at the sunny Fort Lauderdale airport in the middle of a cold New York winter was a first-time experience for me. Shelly picked me up and took me directly to the yacht to meet the others who worked as crew. We discussed how many shows per week she projected I'd be able to do-- possibly two or three; we'd leave it an open-ended agreement and just see how it goes. At $400.00 a pop for up to three shows a week, I was reeling with anticipation. Shelly moved me into a hotel at their expense. Within three weeks, I was living with her.

~

"Hello, my name is Philippe Junot," said the lean, well-tanned genteel man with a heavy French accent.

No, I couldn't believe this. Was this really happening? Only a short time before, I was killing time, sitting in that Wall Street firm's shitter, marveling at ritzy photos of this guy and his wife, Princess Caroline of Monaco, in the society pages. And now here I am—face-to-face with him on a yacht in Florida. And I was going to be singing for him!

Smiling widely, I reached out to shake his hand as I introduced myself, "Hi, I'm Jerry Castaldo, of the Castaldo's from New York; nice to meet you." I had spontaneously assigned myself a pedigree!

Philippe had arrived early. There was no one else on the yacht besides the two of us, standing aft in the outdoor lounge. I was setting up my equipment and he was making himself a drink near the bar of this elegant 112-foot mahogany-wooded yacht, which was the sister ship to the Presidential yacht *Sequoia*.

He invited me to stop what I was doing and have a drink with him. Of course—given my history--it would be a mistake for me to accept an invitation to imbibe. But how could I refuse?

~

Soon thereafter, during a rapidly dialed phone call to my mom in New York, I excitedly recounted these and other amazing events that were happening to me; I said that now maybe my life was going to be akin to that of someone like Andrew Stein. She gently counseled that I shouldn't get used to this extravagant lifestyle. She was trying to protect me from ultimate disappointment. She went on to remind me that we were from a different social class, and that even though it all felt very real to me, I may just be somewhat of an imposter playing a temporary role; I'd always be in danger of losing it all at the whim of my "keepers." I vehemently protested and said to her, "You're wrong!"

The delightful, intoxicating atmosphere in which I was living continued until one morning Shelly and I awoke to the sight of a brand new silver sports car parked right in front of her condo. It was adorned with a giant, shiny red ribbon. The card, neatly tucked under the windshield wiper, simply said, "Happy Birthday, Shelly. Love, Cecil."

Cecil Alderman was a wealthy entrepreneur in his early 60's who had a family back in his native Switzerland but spent a lot of time in the US. He was friends with the owners of this yacht, who were based in Dallas, Texas, and he had gotten to know Shelly through them. Although she swore to me that Cecil was simply her mentor, over time it became clear to me that he was also her benefactor. She had unlimited funds to buy anything and go anywhere she wanted. Of course, my being on the periphery allowed me to enjoy the fruits of his labor, too. So after she explained to me that this wasn't a romance and that she had never slept with him, my jealously eased. She'd even stated to me that he had some kind of injury that prevented him from having sex anyway, and that made me feel better, too. Hindsight is twenty-twenty, though.

"Listen, Jerry--I have to go to New York with Cecil this weekend. There's an event at Regines that he has to attend," Shelly said softly to me, as if to break it to me gently.

This was bullshit. There'd been a few other times that she had to run up to New York, leaving me alone in the condo wondering what the hell was going on. I mean, how stupid must I have been to fall for this?

Shelly went on to say, "Here are some credit cards and the car keys for the Supra."

Great! She was buying me off. Last time it was the "Rock and Roll Hall of Fame Awards" at The Waldorf; the time before that it was a party for Ahmet Ertegun, founder and head of Atlantic Records.

Fuck this, I thought.

~

While Shelly was in New York that weekend, I couldn't help but visualize what must be happening up there. I thought: *What an asshole I've been for allowing this to go on for the past months.* I started processing a litany of depressing memories.

Just the week before this, some of the owners had left their wives behind and had come to Florida for a dinner party on the yacht. I was to sing, and I'd thought it would be a routine evening. When I saw several women boarding that obviously weren't the wives of these men, I realized what was going on. They were high-end call girls. Shelly told me that she needed to actually be a guest herself at this particular party, and it was weird for me to be singing there in the background while I could spy into the dining room watching them all booze it up and eat. After a while, everyone disappeared and I concluded that now they were all in the separate bedrooms onboard. My heart really sank, though, when I realized that Shelly was gone, too. I stopped the music and started walking around to the front of the yacht. No Shelly. I went to the upper deck. No Shelly.

I was crushed and I wanted to flee, but we were now under way and miles from shore. I found a chair on the upper deck and sat stoically, although I wanted to break down. When we got back to shore, there was silence for the drive home. I wouldn't speak to her. She finally pulled over alongside the beach and admitted to me what I'd already suspected. She had procured the girls for those married men. She was the madam. She didn't offer an explanation as to why I couldn't find her for a half hour, and I didn't ask. I didn't want to know.

With Shelly now in New York for the weekend, and me here alone in the condo, all of these thoughts and memories swirling inside my head became unbearable. I was free all weekend to do what I wanted. I had the sports car, money, access to the yacht, and access to half a dozen of Shelly's floozy friends that I could call to party with. I'd observed in the past that these girls had no particular allegiance to her. I dressed nattily, headed out the door and straight to a cocktail lounge.

~

Hours later, I found myself lying uncomfortably on my stomach under a parked car in a huge parking lot, the back of my head only inches from the drive train. It was pouring rain, but I would not emerge from this hiding place until I was sure. Until I was sure that the police who were looking for me had given up.

Shelly's beautiful new car was destroyed after I'd lost control, spun out, and crashed. I was drunk and I didn't have a license, so I got out and ran. Now, I lay there-- wet, shivering, and determined to break it off with her when she got back.

Three days later, while I limply boarded a flight back to New York with great dejection; I winced hard as it struck me that I'd soon be back on the sidewalks again, singing for handouts.

Jerry Seinfeld Offers Me Hope!

Summer 1984–Age 25

#1 song on the radio: "Ghostbusters"--Ray Parker Jr.

Jerry Seinfeld turned to the cute female comedian standing next to him at the bar and said, "I'd like you to meet Jerry Castaldo, and I'm telling you right now-- this guy is going to be the biggest thing in show business."

This ringing endorsement-- coming from a comedian of whom I was in awe--had me floating about for days. It was so gratifying to finally have someone of note in the entertainment world recognize the hard work I was putting in. I'd been making all of his New York shows, and this night I was standing here with him at New York's Village Gate nightclub before he was to go on and do his set.

A couple of years before, I'd seen Seinfeld make one of his first appearances on "Late Night with David Letterman." He was starting to gain notoriety as he had already scored very well both on "The Tonight Show" and the "Merv Griffin Show." I was impressed with his material and with his delivery. I'd been studying countless other new and established comedians, both "live" and on VHS tape, but he stood out--especially in the clubs, where he didn't rely on the shock value of profanity or sexual situations to elicit laughs. I noticed that many comics working the clubs couldn't even get five clean minutes for TV.

At one point during his interview with Letterman, Seinfeld mentioned that he lived on the Upper West Side of Manhattan. A light went off in my head! Maybe I can get to know him and eventually become his opening act. From reading the show biz weekly *Variety,* I'd gleaned that singers and comics were often paired for shows. Fingering through the pages of the enormous New York phonebook, I found an address for a J. Seinfeld in the west 80's. There wasn't a phone number listed with the address. Hell, I didn't even know if I had the right person! I did know, however, that to show up in person would put me just one step below a stalker. So I methodically assembled my 20-page press book, threw in my 8 X 10 headshot, and mailed it off. I waited patiently for a reply.

Nothing.

A few months later, it was quite surprising to me when Seinfeld himself walked into the health-club where I was teaching. It was a second-floor gym above a supermarket, with a stunning, birds-eye view of the famed Beacon Theatre directly across the street.

"Hi Jerry," I stammered. "I'm Jerry Castaldo. I'm the guy who sent you that press book to your apartment. Did you get it?" I asked.

Seinfeld confirmed that yes, he did get it, but only recently. He explained that he now was living out in LA most of the time. We talked a bit about our both performing at Pips back in Brooklyn, and I told him my idea about opening for him. He gave me his California address and phone number, and told me to let him think about what he might be able to do. I refrained from calling him during the next few days. I wanted to appear motivated, but I didn't want to become a pest.

Incidentally, everyone to whom I would tell this story back then-- about my meeting this up-and-coming comedian I'd seen on network television--would then ask me, "Who's Jerry Steinfeld?" I had to keep correcting them, saying, "No, Seinfeld--Jerry Seinfeld, not Steinfeld. You've never heard of him?" People would just shrug their shoulders, clearly underwhelmed, and reply, "No."

In the few years that I'd been out there in the trenches, auditioning, I'd made some inroads. The Brooklyn Arts and Cultural Association (BACA), for instance, had picked me up and had me doing my one-hour shows at parks, libraries, and various outdoor events. BACA exec Chuck Reichenthal was instrumental in getting me these gigs after he'd seen me perform in a showcase one night in downtown Brooklyn.

Every year they'd sponsor the "Welcome Back to Brooklyn" event to crown a home-grown celebrity as "King." We were once fortunate enough to have comedian Dom Deluise accept the invitation for him to be so honored. It was thrilling for me to be part of this huge event and to have my photo featured in the New York *Daily News* publicizing it. Quite disturbing to me, though, was the extreme disappointment I suffered after talking to Deluise. I appealed to him to help me, much the way I did with Seinfeld. He took my photo and resume from me, and promised to call me that very night to talk about my future. Mary Lou and I were back together again and she witnessed this surreal exchange. Afterwards, she and I were hugging each other and jumping up and down; we both thought: *This is it! My break!* We waited, giddy with excitement, all evening near the phone. The call never came.

Forging on, I had other small, incremental successes that kept my dream alive. By now I'd logged multiple appearances at Freddy's Supper Club on the Upper East Side. There, I would cross paths with such well-known recording stars as Maureen McGovern, who also performed there regularly. (Many years later I'd host and open a show for McGovern, in a huge theatre down south.) I was able to get the *New York Post's* cabaret critic, Curt Davis, to attend my show numerous times during those years, too. His first reviews of me were quite innocuous. Eventually, though, he was won over. Davis never praised the power and range of my singing voice, but he championed my ability as an all-around entertainer who was fun to watch. It would take several more years of working before I'd develop real vocal chops. The Freddy's appearances also helped get my photo into the widely-circulated *New York Magazine.*

~

"Look at this, it's Jerry Castaldo! Unbelievable! What the heck are you doing here? What is this?" These were the exasperated words coming from Jerry Seinfeld's mouth as he slowed from a walk to a dead stop directly in front of me, his eyes wide and face contorted in a strange combination of curiosity and wonderment. I was smiling at him and continued singing.

He'd just gotten off a subway train coming from Manhattan and was casually strolling down the tree-lined residential street, both hands in his pockets, on his way to his gig. I'd actually seen him way in the distance and I'd started chuckling to myself because I knew he'd recognize me once he got closer.

Singer Vic Damone was headlining an outdoor concert at Brooklyn's Midwood Field, and Seinfeld was the opening act. Senator Marty Markowitz (who is now Brooklyn Borough President) presented a concert series every summer and I'd gone up to his office headquarters to try to get on the bill with Seinfeld and Damone.

I stopped singing into the microphone and paused the pre-recorded music tracks that were blaring from my street-show setup. "I'm opening for you opening for Vic Damone," I declared loudly to Seinfeld, still smiling widely.

Seinfeld had been cordial with me ever since we'd met, and I'd hang around with him at his shows when I could. I'd call him in California from time to time, too. But the truth was, there was no way that I was going to become his regular opening-act. He was with the APA Talent Agency in Manhattan at that time, and my calls to his agent Lou Viola went unreturned. Now, here I was, set up outside of the entrance gate to this huge football field where the concert was to start soon, and I was singing-- not to an assembled captive audience, but to the audience members as they were coming in to be seated! This was the best that Senator Markowitz said he could do for me.

"I have to hand it to you, Jerry," Seinfeld touted.

After engaging in some small talk, Seinfeld and I shook hands and he continued in to the field area. I flipped a few switches and resumed performing.

Yes, I felt like an asshole; yes I probably looked like an asshole, too. But still, at least I somehow felt connected.

Connected to this business of show.

~

"One, two, three—again!" I urged my star client Andrew Stein—briskly executing bent-leg sit-ups--to keep up with my cadence.

While still Borough President, Stein had become the Democratic nominee for Congress in the "Silk Stocking District" on the Upper East Side, running against incumbent Republican Bill Green. He informed me that our workout schedule would now have to start earlier--at 5:15 am--because the campaign was on.

No longer did I need to work at the health clubs or travel from building to building in the predawn hours to train people in their homes. Andrew Stein was now my one and only client. This was because my show schedule was picking up. Besides the BACA shows, I was now performing at senior-citizen centers and private long-term care facilities. The money was good and programs were presented in the mornings, afternoons, and evenings. So if you really hustled--which I did,--you could rack up financially. Of course, it was still a paltry sum compared to the "real" showbiz pay scale, but very comfortable compared to typical blue-collar earnings. In the coming years I would wind up averaging about 300 one-hour shows of this type per year—and one year I logged 347 shows! And performing these kind of shows made more sense financially than working for a percentage of the door at the Manhattan cabarets-- where no performers ever really made any money unless you were a big "name" draw. After pouring all of your own money into promotion, you'd wind up having your friends, family, and colleagues as the audience-- and the clubs made all of the money.

"One, two, three--again!" As I continued to count off the reps for Stein, he kept looking at me strangely. I ignored it at first, but then I kept glancing back at him and I'd catch him staring at me again. I finally asked, "What's the matter? Is everything OK?" He just glared at me and kept exercising. I persisted: "What?"

He stopped, sat up, looked at me with his eyebrows angled down, forehead furrowed, and harshly asked, "What do you think you are doing writing the Governor's daughter and using my name?"

Shit! How the hell did he know that I'd written a letter to Maria Cuomo, daughter of then-Governor Mario Cuomo? I immediately started retracing my steps mentally on the spot, trying to figure it out.

I'd read an interview that Maria Cuomo gave for *GQ Magazine* where she revealed that she was single and looking for a relationship. Mary Lou was now seeing someone else anyway, so I found an address for Maria Cuomo and wrote her a long, hand-written letter telling her all about me. To get her attention, I mentioned that I was the personal fitness coach of Manhattan Borough President Andrew J. Stein. Unbeknownst to me, however, Maria Cuomo knew Andrew Stein's daughter from school—they both were then attending Boston University--so word of my letter traveled straight back to Stein.

I meekly tried to explain, "Look, Andrew, I was very respectful in the letter. I just thought she was pretty and that I might have a chance, so I wrote to her."

He just shook his head from side to side as if he was really pissed off, while at the same time telling me not to do things like that anymore. But I could swear that I caught a little bit of a smile break on his face as he was turning away. Shortly thereafter, rumors abounded that Governor Cuomo might run for President and I thought: *Wow, imagine that? If she'd gone out with me and we'd clicked, my father-in-law might have been President of the United States!* Maria Cuomo went on to marry millionaire shoe designer Kenneth Cole.

another fares + jump moment

"Anthony? Hi, it's Shelly Malone. My boyfriend Jerry and I want to know what time to meet you." Sitting there in my apartment watching Shelly on a call with critically acclaimed writer Anthony Haden-Guest, finalizing our dinner plans with him, clinched for me the feeling that I was once again on the fast track.

Shelly had made multiple long-distance overtures to get back together with me and I'd finally given in. She'd even written a long letter to my mom proclaiming her love for me. And ours was certainly a whirlwind reunion; I often flew down to Florida to see Shelly, and sometimes she flew up to Manhattan to see me. I truly wanted to believe that Cecil Alderman was indeed—as Shelly claimed-- only her mentor. This was made a bit easier for me to accept because Shelly and I had access to Cecil's spacious penthouse apartment on York Avenue, on Manhattan's Upper East Side. And we put it to good use. Shelly would even leave me the keys so that I could use Cecil's apartment when she was back down in Florida. I was enjoying myself. It felt like my life was all limos, nightclubs, and fancy restaurants. And none of this was costing me a penny.

Alcoholics and drug addicts all seem to have this one common peculiarity. When things are going badly for us and life gets tough, we "use" in order to get through the tough times. But, paradoxically, when things are going great and we are happy, we "use" in order to celebrate. Both scenarios ultimately bring us to the same place: a life that is unmanageable.

I'd never been a fan of soap-opera stories, but before long it felt as if I were becoming embroiled in one. Shelly had called me this one week saying she wouldn't be able to make it up to New York, but I sensed that something was wrong; she sounded nervous during our talk. That Saturday, I made repeated calls to her home in Florida and to the yacht, but I could not find her. This brought back bad memories for me of the "Night of the Prostitutes" escapade. I finally got someone from the yacht on the phone, and I pressed him to tell me where Shelly was. I was shocked to hear that she'd flown up to New York to meet with Cecil.

Liar! I thought, as I felt the sting of blistering emotional pain consume me. Why was she doing this to me?

This confusing rollercoaster-ride of feelings that I was on with her was going to end--right now! I jumped into a cab, headed to Cecil's apartment, and asked the doorman if Cecil Alderman--whom I'd never met--was at home. It was now late afternoon. The doorman told me that Mr. Alderman and a tall blond woman had just left. I felt despair.

Taking up a position across the street from Cecil's building, I alternated between sitting on the sloping edge of a fire hydrant and standing, as the night wore on. Ten o'clock, eleven o'clock... it was now raining..... At about one am, a sleek, chauffeured black Lincoln Town Car crept up to the front of the building. The agile doorman rushed toward it while opening an umbrella. I watched a big, fat, balding man awkwardly waddle from the car toward the lobby--not even waiting for his companion, who was still back in the car. I stepped forward, closer to the curb and out of the shadows, as I watched a windswept Shelly finally emerge from the Lincoln. Since the doorman was busy shielding Cecil, and since the driver didn't bother to get out, Shelly had to turn toward the street to slam the car door shut. At that moment, we made direct eye contact with each other. She stood frozen while we just stared for a few seconds. I then turned and walked away.

Slinking home with my tail between my legs, I felt betrayed and hurt. I lay in bed for the next two hours, my mind racing. I couldn't take this shit anymore! I found myself rushing to find a pen and paper; I feverishly started writing a letter to Shelly demanding that she stay out of my life. I put it in an envelope, got another cab, and headed back uptown to Cecil's building-- their "love nest." No longer was I feeling hurt; by now I was blind with rage and fury. Concealed uncomfortably under my left arm, nestled tight into my armpit, was a huge claw hammer that I'd taken from my apartment.

The doorman knew my face from my frequent comings-and-goings in the previous months when I was using the apartment. So he did not question me when I waved to him and walked straight in through the lobby to the elevator bank. I made sure he could not see the bulge of my weapon distorting the line of my light rain coat. That old familiar "fight or flight" body-twitching was occurring now as my anger intensified.

Upon arriving at the apartment door—it was now about four in the morning--I ripped the hammer from its hiding place, wound up like a baseball pitcher, and with all my might, started beating the steel door repeatedly like a wild man. I was yelling over and over, "Shelly, take this fucking note! Open this door. Take it, take it!" I knew I had limited time to get out of the building before the police would arrive; I was sure the other tenants on the floor would be dialing 911 in response to the deafening sound of steel on steel colliding.

Shelly then started yelling back through the closed door, "Okay, okay, just wait, wait one minute." I stopped banging the now-pockmarked door and heard the chain-lock slip on. I impatiently watched the door crack open a few inches.

"Here, take this letter! And leave me the fuck alone!" I demanded as I shoved the letter through the narrow opening.

I ran back to the elevator, went down to the lobby, passed the confused doorman, and headed out into the now pouring rain. I walked the entire 68 blocks home, sopping wet and unsuccessfully trying to stifle my tears.

~

Many years later, Shelly's highly publicized and violent death in West Virginia's wealthy blue-blood country would fascinate the entire country. Her puzzling and mysterious demise even became the subject of a national television program.

That last year that we were together; I'd known that Shelly had been called to Dallas on more than one occasion to testify against some of the powerful business people who owned the yacht. She had told me that she feared some sort of retaliation--even though she was just telling the truth, under oath, about how she managed the yacht's books. The yacht's owners were later linked to one member of the "Keating Five"--five US

Senators accused of corruption, who ignited a major political scandal as part of the Savings and Loan crisis of the late 1980's. I'm not implying anything here; I'm just stating the facts. Any speculation on my part regarding Shelly's murder has never been substantiated in a court of law.

It was while I was coming out of the shower one morning in the mid-'90s that I heard from the TV in my bedroom the familiar voice of actor Robert Stack. He was doing a promo spot for his show "Unsolved Mysteries," which was to air the following week. Hearing him say, "The unsolved case of the death of Shelly Malone," made me do a double-take; I ran, naked and wet, out of the bathroom to the television set. The commercial was already over by then, so I called the network and managed to get a production assistant on the phone. Yes, he confirmed, this was indeed a Shelly Malone of Fort Lauderdale, Florida. When the episode finally aired, my family and I watched it and were flabbergasted. Afterward, I thought to myself, "Did they really have to show Shelly's morgue photos?"

The Chippendales Shows

Fall 1986–Age 26

#1 song on the radio: "You Give Love A Bad Name"–Bon Jovi

"Good evening everyone and welcome to Magique, home of Chippendales. Tonight we present to you *Jerry C,"* the corny sounding DJ announced through the club's booming PA system.

Yeah, welcome to the fuckin' freak show, I was thinking as I jumped out into the spotlight like some greasy Euro-trash club-kid gyrating for the audience. There was only one major problem: there was hardly any audience!

This weird promoter, who went by the single name of "Dante," had booked me to do four separate shows at these parties heralding in some low-budget Indie films. My performances, on four consecutive Wednesdays, would start at midnight. I'd written some dance-pop songs and I was to sing three of them to kick off each of the night's festivities. Before 11 pm, the club was filled with just women who'd be there to watch the male strip show. I would come out later, after the strip show was finished, as *Jerry C.* This certainly was a departure from "The Great American Songbook."

The promoter requested that I dress in this baby-blue velour outfit, wearing sneakers and a bright yellow windbreaker; I looked like a friggin' bumble-bee pulsating under the strobe lights. Even weirder-- there were several giant video screens all around the club, high up near the ceiling. To my utter disgust, as I danced I could

151

see on each screen what looked like multiple human-sized "schmears" of mustard quivering in sync!

Having to push and weave through the throng of women while trying to get into the overcrowded dressing room each night was also a mess. These big, muscular---and by now sweaty and shining-- male strippers would all be in the dressing room with dozens of drunk, middle-aged women fawning all over them. It was almost impossible to get near the lockers to put my stuff away. This decadent scene was topped off with a putrid smell-- a disgusting mix of cigarette smoke, booze, cheap perfume, and desperation! The sad fact for me was that after all of this hullabaloo, the place would then pretty much empty out. And the few people, who stuck around after the strip show was over, when I had to sing, could not have cared less about me.

"Hey Jerry, your girlfriend is here," said the club manager to me one night after I was finally "in costume" and ready to go on.

I thought, *Oh No....* Initially, I had been excited about doing these shows--before I had any idea how terrible they would be. So I'd informed a few friends and family about them. And now, to my dismay, some of them were actually showing up to witness this circus.

I'd been dating a really sweet girl named Gabrielle Robbins, but I was embarrassed that she was here. It wasn't only because it was such a lame booking, but Gabrielle was from a respected show-business family and she herself was an actress and a great singer. Her brother, actor Tim Robbins, was at that time starring in his first major Hollywood film, and he later went on to win Academy Awards for both directing and acting. I was mortified that she was going to see this.

~

After Andrew Stein was unable to beat his opponent and win the congressional seat, he focused in on becoming New York's City Council President. This position was just one step below that of then Mayor, Ed Koch. I was excited to enlist in Stein's campaign and lend a hand. He and I would drive together to the outer boroughs where he'd speak at various sites. At some of the bigger events, I was the MC and would warm up the crowd with a few songs before Stein would come out and address them. To help us with running the sound equipment at these appearances, I was given the OK to bring in an industrious young musician from Chicago named Tom Kochan.

Tom and his actress wife, Cheryl Stern, had moved to New York some years before, and it was very clear to me that they both worked tirelessly in building their careers. Tom, an excellent musician proficient at several different instruments, was also an arranger and music producer with a then state-of-the-art recording studio. He'd also tour the world as conductor for music-great Trini Lopez. I'd found Tom through a trade paper when I sought to make my first demos. I'd funnel time-payments to him in "nickels and dimes" from what I made singing on the street. When I'd gotten the Revlon tour, he was brought in to produce pristine music tracks for the shows. Shortly after that, when I was finally able to come up with a substantial amount of money to invest in my act, he did the arrangements for me; thanks to his arrangements, I was able to perform my entire show with up to a 12-piece orchestra. I'm thrilled that Tom later went on to win an Emmy Award for composing, and that his wife, Cheryl, performs regularly on Broadway; she is currently appearing in the Tony Award-winning revival of *La Cage Au Folles*!

While I was working with Stein one early Monday morning, he asked, "Do you know who I had dinner with yesterday?" I shook my head and asked, "Who?"

"Frank Sinatra," he revealed.

Hearing that, I was tempted to confess everything and tell him about my "Frank Sinatra at Carnegie Hall" night of carnage. But even though I felt close to him, I was keeping a deep, dark secret that I wished I could share but knew that I could not—that I was an addict.

There'd been other times he'd told me fascinating stories, too. Once he'd told me about going sailing with Kennedy-family matriarch Ethel Kennedy up near the compound in Hyannis Port. With them were several other members of the Kennedy clan, and two dogs. The mind-boggling thing was that she'd suggested they undertake this grand adventure amidst a raging rainstorm--and not one person protested as they all walked along the slippery, jagged rocks!

I sensed that Stein was quite excited to be able to mix with such company. To me, of course, *he* was the celebrity--although he was so down-to-earth. He'd even appear somewhat star-struck himself at times. I remember occasions when, while we'd be working out, he'd point to the television and say, "See that guy? He's my close friend." The first time he did that, he was pointing to a then-unknown Donald Trump. Later, he'd say, "Jerry, see that guy? I'm good friends with him." When I looked, I saw the then-wonder-kid prosecutor Rudolph Giuliani. Celebrated actress Shirley MacLaine and Stein were best friends, too, and would be seen around town together. It was all so interesting for me to be a part of this in some way—although I still essentially felt like an outsider.

Andrew Stein went on to win the City Council President seat and I was extended a personal invitation to the Inaugural Ball Gala. This was an ideal opportunity for me to not only to celebrate the victory of a good man whom I admired, but also for me to mingle and develop my own valuable connections for the future. Back yet again with my girlfriend Mary Lou, she was excited about our attending, too, as she contemplated what to wear.

That should have been a great day for me. Instead, however, I got high and wound up missing this most important event. Worse yet, I'd started calling in a substitute trainer for him because I was often incapacitated.

I'd had several great years with Andrew Stein. But now--because I'd started to display outward signs of erratic behavior due to my being imprisoned by addiction—I was dismissed from his life forever.

Chaos Ensues as I Slowly Unravel

"And don't come back, you shithead!" yelled one of the two burly stagehands who had just violently ejected me into the back alley, sending me airborne and crashing onto the concrete. As I lay there, feeling intense pain in my knees and elbows that had taken the brunt, I remembered seeing something like this happen in an old movie. It was called a "Bum's Rush," and it was the way unruly drunks were thrown out from saloons. Tonight, I was the bum.

I'd come to the backstage door of this Broadway theatre to visit my friend Robert Billig, or Bob as he's known to most, a veteran musical conductor who was working on a production called *Song and Dance.* The show was already underway, and I don't recall anything other than my being so "out of it" that I could barely walk straight when I'd arrived in the alley. I planned to go to Bob's dressing room and wait for him until the show was over. I'd found a way to pry open the backstage door, which had no outside handle, and then I'd pulled it open with too much force, causing it to make a startling boom. Several stagehands immediately confronted me; we started scuffling and we all started yelling. I can remember seeing that the star of the show, Bernadette Peters, was onstage and nervously glancing over her left shoulder while she was in the middle of singing a song, trying to figure out what the commotion was about.

I'd met Bob a few years before when he was the musical director for the Off Broadway hit, *Little Shop of Horrors*. It was during that two-year period when I was temporarily sober. We'd become friends. In fact, he even once agreed to play piano for me on a local cable-TV show despite the fact that he was a "name" in his field and I was then basically just a "street singer." He was, and is, very well respected in the theatre community.

With my out-of-control behavior now being what it was, I realized that I was in jeopardy of losing yet another good friend.

The national "crack" cocaine epidemic had by then started to take hold. Looking back, I wonder how I ever could have allowed myself to even try something that was being called the most addictive drug in history. Before long, there were crack-head girls running around my apartment topless, and I was withdrawing cash advances on my American Express card in shameful amounts. In one two-week period I advanced myself four thousand dollars for drugs—while losing so much weight that my clothes were literally falling off of me. I also stupidly allowed one of these girls to inject heroin into my veins with a shared needle.

Remnants of family and real friends who were barely holding on with me had often bandied about the terms "recovery," "treatment," and "rehab"--and I resented them for it. *Rehab,* I told myself, *was for the weak. For people who have no discipline. Not for me! I'm strong. I get high and drink at times after long periods of being sober only because "I want to."*

This is what I had convinced myself of; that's what I firmly believed for years. I'd gone to rehab a few times because I was ordered to do so by the courts, but I'd never gone voluntarily. It was somewhere about this time that I started to suspect, though... that maybe I was wrong.

Ironically, in this period I was hired to do an on-camera silent-bit in a commercial for the National Council on Alcoholism. I had to sit at a piano and simulate playing-- and I'm sure I smelled of alcohol. My auditions were suffering, too. I once wasted my time driving all the way to Boston to audition for a play when I was obviously hung over.

Always my angelic savior, even though Mary Lou would occasionally need to distance herself from me, she would always eventually reappear, and help me in any way that she could. But by now, I seemed beyond help.

~

Jerry Seinfeld held his hand up toward me; arm rigidly straight as if he were a traffic cop directing me to halt. "No Jerry, no, not now. You gotta leave, I'm goin' on right now," he said sternly.

The old Caroline's Comedy Club on Eighth Avenue was a hotbed of popular comics during the comedy boom of the 1980's. I'd been able to jump up onstage to sing impromptu a few times before some comedians started their sets, "opening" for them, but club owner Caroline Hirsch wasn't big on having singers onstage. The audiences who came here were there to laugh.

I knew Seinfeld was booked that night and I'd left him a message on his answering machine telling him that I'd be there, and I got to the club right before curtain time. I confidently announced to the manager that I was a personal friend of Seinfeld's and was led backstage.

I sputtered back unintelligibly at Seinfeld, as if my mouth were full of marbles, "No, no, Jerry; here, it's ok; I'm leavin'. I wuz just bringin' you my new tape of songs."

By now the bouncer was in the dressing room with us, both of his hands on my arms as he escorted me out.

I squeezed in quickly before I was completely out of the room, "Awright, awright! I'll call you, Jerry; I'll call you!"

Fuck him! I thought as I stepped out of the club and onto the sidewalk.

My mind had become so warped and twisted that now I was blaming Seinfeld for not wanting to be my friend. But who in their right mind would want to even know me? I was an embarrassment, the scum of the earth, a scourge of society.

Death was becoming a viable option to me. I'd failed so many times, had so many false starts; things seemed hopeless. I was continuing to lose family, friends, jobs, and my own self-respect. *Why couldn't I fix myself? Am I really so weak after all? Is this how it's going to be for the rest of my life?*

That night, for the very first time since I was a religious 12 year old boy, I actually knelt down and prayed.

The Giant Monster Comes for Me at Night

Winter 1987--Age 28

#1 song on the radio: "Faith"—George Michael

Do you remember your first dream? Think for a moment. What age were you when you awoke from your nightly slumber, shocked, fascinated, and endlessly curious as you reflected on what had just happened to you or to someone else in one of your first dreams or nightmares?

For me, the time that I actually started clearly remembering my dreams is exactly when particularly terrifying visions started. I was about five years old. The torture that this one nightmare inflicted upon me continued consistently until I was almost 30. It was only then-- alone in my Manhattan apartment during a severe three-day withdrawal period from barbiturates, one of my many attempts to shake my addiction--that I finally met the ferocious, bloodthirsty demon eye-to-eye.

Of course, over the years I also experienced many nice dreams--like sex dreams and flying dreams—along with various more-or-less "regular" nightmare dreams. But the particularly spine-tingling, chilling nightmare that I'm talking about here can now bask in the success of its 20 plus-year run--enviable by any Hollywood standard.

The nightmare was always the same. Even as I turned into an adolescent and then into a young man in my 20's, in this recurring dream I was still only about five years old. I was always in a frenzied race to escape the scary being who was "out to kill me."

161

Jerry Castaldo

During my turbulent teens, when I was buying up books en masse from the self-help sections of New York bookstores, I decided to investigate. Before the age of the Internet, it was much harder to comb through literature for learning and research. Nothing was at your fingertips like it is today. You had to either go to a library or actually buy a book. I did both. And what many books claimed was that people who had a lot of nightmares were very creative and artistic. I thought: *Wow, great! What a relief, now I can be assured that something good is coming out of all of this.* Hey, since I truly wanted to be the quintessential Renaissance Man who creates many different things in many different disciplines, then being told I was creative and artistic seemed perfect!

I'm tempted to say that this giant monster chasing after me in these nightmares, who seemed to stand about four stories high, was sort of like King Kong. But to tell you the truth, when I used to watch the King Kong movie, I empathized with Kong, I felt sorry for him. In fact, I could actually feel a kind of "love" for him; I used to want to help and protect him as he suffered the many injustices dealt him during the film. Only later--after I confronted the monster-of-my-nightmares during our very last encounter--would I realize how significant this King Kong association might be.

Our four-room apartment--that we lived in from the time that I was born until I was ten-years-old (when we moved out of Park Slope to the Bensonhurst section of Brooklyn)--was what they call a railroad apartment. The four rooms ran in a straight line, with two bedroom windows at the front of the building, and one single window at the back of the building, facing a small yard.

You had to walk through one room to get to the next. The front windows of this third-floor bedroom provided just enough height for us to see over the roof of the building across the street, and provided us with a clear view of the Statue of Liberty. The actual NYC skyline was obscured by buildings to the right of us.

The front bedroom was my parents' room, and the next bedroom in was for my brother Ken and I. We slept on one of those twin pop-up beds that allows for storing one mattress down under the other when one was not in use. Lots of exposed springs, mechanical and noisy; and don't catch your fingers in it while operating it!

Did you ever think about how desolate and unpopulated some nightmares can be? In that recurring nightmare, I was the only one around.

Where are the other people? Where are the other victims? Why is it only me here?

It would be the middle of the night. In the dream, I would awaken to some kind of horrible roaring sound. Think Godzilla, Kong, and throw in some other wild African animals. I'd get out of bed. *Where is my brother? Where are my parents?*

I didn't see anybody. I'd walk to the door and descend the two flights of stairs to the street, looking for my family. The sound of the unseen monster was getting louder. It seemed to be coming from the deserted dead-end street that was one block to the left from where our building was. It was coming from the cemetery!

Yes, it was coming from behind the foreboding eight-foot tall, black wrought-iron fence that separated the street from the massive, five-hundred acre Green-Wood Cemetery. Although it was always creepy to me, it actually holds National Historic Landmark status. Resting there are almost three quarter of a million of the dead. Conductor Leonard Bernstein, journalist Edward R. Murrow, and actor Frank Morgan (who played the Wizard in "The Wizard of Oz") are among the many notables buried there today.

Once I was down on the sidewalk in front of my building, the roaring sound coming from the cemetery would get louder and louder. Then I would start to see some sort of movement which, although blurry, convinced me that this monster was now making its way toward me. And what was its intent? To get me--and presumably kill me or eat me; I didn't really know. I'd run into our apartment building's tiny vestibule, which had two entrance doors--one door that swung in, right from the street, and then another door, about nine feet in. I would be desperately holding the first door shut while the monster was trying to push it in to get me. Then I'd make it through the second door and do the same thing, again trying to hold it back. Then, I'd let go of the door to start running up the first flight of stairs, but my legs were heavy and wouldn't move fast enough. I'd feel it grab me from behind....

And then, terrified, I would wake up.

At twenty-eight-years-old—struggling through this one really hellish drug-detoxification period--I found myself there once again. I was deep in a delirious dream state.

The monster, as always, was in pursuit of me. I could hear it coming after me, but could not really see it.

This time, though, I decided—after some 20 years of suffering this nightmare--I would face it.

Just as I was about to let go of the second entrance door--to try running up the stairs and away from the monster--I stopped.

I gathered up all of the courage that I could find. I gulped in a very deep breath, widened my eyes, and forced myself to quickly—almost violently--spin around to see "who" or "what" this thing actually was.

I'd fight it to the death, right now. I was tired of running. I looked hard and unflinching.

It was me.

wow!!

Death by Subway Train

December 17th, 1988--Age 29

#1 song on the radio: "Look Away"—Chicago

I thought to myself, "I can't believe that this is how it's all going to end; my life is over." The subway station at Union Square-14th Street in Manhattan was a noisy labyrinth of interconnecting city train lines that had always been fun to navigate by foot. It was great exercise. Whether running up or down the concrete staircases to make train connections on my way to work, to an acting audition, or to meet my drug dealers, I always found that particular station exciting, vibrant, and full of life. After growing up in Brooklyn, it was a personal victory for me, a few years earlier at age 25, to had made it over the Brooklyn Bridge and actually live on my own in Manhattan. My apartment was right down the street from this very station.

Standing on the platform of the "N" line, I stared down at the filthy black track-bed. A small rat was running parallel to the rail. It always smelled like--I don't know; I can't describe it--electricity or something down there underground. Subways in NYC have an unmistakable aroma. Not necessarily a bad smell. Actually it had become sort of pleasant to me--familiar, ever since my dad took my brother and me to Coney Island by subway when we were kids. I remember the station there had cotton-candy shops and hot-peanut stands, as well as vendors offering candy-coated apples and other goodies. Maybe from then on I had always associated those sweet scents with the basic subway smell.

At this moment, staring down at the tracks, I realized that this was indeed the end for me—there was nothing else to live for. I had never made it to the big time in show business and probably never would, despite many years of hard work and dedication. By now I was struggling to pay my bills and not lose my apartment. And most distressing of all, I couldn't kick the drugs that provided me with relief from the round-the-clock stress and anxiety that I experienced throughout my adult life.

I looked down the tunnel to see if a train's headlights were approaching yet. And that made me start to cry. I looked down the black, cavernous hole and saw nothing.

I had wanted to be an athlete, and in a way I was. I'd run, eat right, lift weights. I had wanted to be a scholar. Well, I read several newspapers each day, subscribed to trade and news magazines, and read self-help books. Books like Dr. Wayne Dyer's "The Sky's The Limit," or L. Ron Hubbard's "The Modern Science of Mental Health" --which is about "Dianetics," and which we now know, via tabloid fodder, is Scientology. I had wanted to be helpful to people, again, almost pious-like since my days as an altar boy. (In fact, I had once even imagined becoming a priest; I actually requested a monogrammed Bible from my mom for my Confirmation gift instead of a bicycle.) I had wanted to be a star, recognized for my many years of singing, songwriting, guitar playing, acting.... And I had wanted the money that comes with such accomplishments.

I wanted, I wanted; I wanted.... But it seemed I had nothing.

I looked down the tracks again and saw lights. "What a fuckin' pussy I am," I thought. *Boo-hoo, poor Jerry, he wants to kill himself just because he can't have what he wants.* I felt like such an asshole, but I also felt somewhat justified because I had had a series of bad breaks over the years. *Or, did I create those bad times myself? Shit, of course I did. How? The fuckin' drugs.*

What I did have, though, I realized, was a family. Maybe we were slightly estranged from one another. But my family loved me. As did my childhood sweetheart, Mary Lou, who I'd started dating in the eighth grade. Over the course of the last 15 years together, she had stood by me throughout many horrible situations that I had created for myself.

I always felt great guilt about Mary Lou having to live through all of those things. Honestly, as I've said before, she was just the most gentle, non-judgmental, truly "good" person I had ever met up until that point in my tumultuous life.

Hearing a high pitched, metallic squeal, I peered down the tunnel again. Lights! Another train was coming into the station. *"Do it now!"*

Do I do it now? I was disgusted with myself. And I cried out loud. There were dozens of people standing on my platform, and on the platform across the way on the other side, the northbound tracks. And some of them, naturally, were now staring at me.

"What the fuck are you looking at?" I taunted at a couple of guys who were wondering why I was sobbing.

"You wanna fuck with me? I'll kill you all!" Flailing my arms, I looked and sounded crazed. No one would dare make eye contact with me or challenge me now. At that moment, I was totally nuts.

It was about eight o'clock on a Tuesday night during the Christmas Holiday season. People were carrying Macy's bags, no doubt filled with gifts they'd be giving to their family and friends the following week; Macy's was the very next stop on the subway line, Herald Square. Mary Lou was back at my apartment. I had just stormed out of there, because we'd been arguing. I was high, and that had upset her because I had stayed clean for about three months--but now I had relapsed again, for like the one-hundredth time. I was angry that she couldn't see that at least I was always trying. Even though I had failed yet again, I would never give up trying.

As the train pulled out from the station and I remained standing there on the platform, I started getting hostile toward myself. "You don't even have the fuckin' guts to do this," I told myself. Maybe it was because I couldn't shake the gruesome thoughts of my previous experience with subway deaths.

Cindy Tarisi—who had been my first girlfriend in sixth grade--had killed herself by jumping in front of a subway train about seven years earlier, when I was 22. On the day that she died, by chance, I was almost at the same spot where she did it. I remember waiting on a Brooklyn-to-Manhattan-bound subway-train platform for about an hour with no train in sight; finally, a transit official came down to tell us all that there'd be no service for a few hours because "someone had fallen to the tracks" at the next station up. Later, I found out that that "someone" who had "fallen" was Cindy. *Had I used that next station up instead of the one I was at, would I have seen her jump? Would I have been able to stop her?*

Another memory. When I was 14 years old, my mother's 28-year-old sister Audrey, who was having a hard time emotionally, came to our apartment and stayed the night with us. The next day, when I was at school, some of the kids were saying that a lady had jumped onto the elevated train tracks; she'd been hit by the train, and pieces of her body had fallen to the street below. When I got home from school and saw my Aunt Ellen comforting my crying mother, I just knew.... We had a closed-casket wake.

There was a pay phone on the platform. I called my apartment, still sobbing, begging Mary Lou not to move out and end our relationship as she had threatened to do, right before I left that evening.

I thought about our history together. A couple of years earlier, before I had gotten my own place in Manhattan, Mary Lou had invited me to live with her in a Brooklyn apartment she had just rented, but I declined. (This was just after my Army stint in Germany; I was living at home again, with my mom.) I didn't want to feel like I was living off of Mary Lou, though, or anybody for that matter and wanted my own place. She had just gotten a great job in the mortgage section of a prominent bank and I was making a low salary working as an instructor at the Jack La Lanne Health Club.

What finally drove me out of my mom's turning-dingy-by-the-day apartment building was what happened one night. While sleeping, I felt something on my chest. It woke me up; I immediately held my breath and froze. "Nah, that can't be a cockroach," I thought. All of a sudden I felt it racing up my chest toward my neck. It *was* a roach! I flung the covers off my body. I swear--I may have actually sprung up toward the friggin' ceiling in my panic to escape, what I thought, was the most disgusting living thing imaginable. I promptly got up and---right then in the middle of the night--went straight over to Mary Lou's new apartment, woke her up and said, "OK, thanks, I'm moving in."

Noisy, windy subway platforms are not exactly the best place to make a desperate, emotional plea from a pay phone during a serious relationship negotiation. (Back in 1988, the only cell phones around were usually found in the cars of people with real money.) But I had to try. "Hello? Mary Lou?" I begged and pleaded with her not to move out of my apartment. Not to go back to the place she used to have, in Brooklyn. It wasn't because I didn't want to live alone. I actually loved having my own place in Manhattan and not having to answer to anyone. But I was traumatized by what had happened the previous summer. I felt responsible for the vicious attack that Mary Lou had suffered, back in her apartment, at the hands of a knife-wielding rapist.

After living with her in that Brooklyn apartment for about two years, I then had moved into the city by myself; she stayed behind. Because of the on-again, off-again level of sobriety that I was exhibiting to her, she didn't tell me about being raped until a week after it had happened to her. A man had climbed in through the kitchen window and made his way into her bedroom while she slept. He straddled her and—holding the knife to her throat--raped her in the very bed in which I used to sleep with her. I know that the rape wasn't "about me," but I too felt angry and helpless when I learned what had happened. It was so hurtful to me that she didn't even tell me until well afterwards. I couldn't help but feel that if I had stayed with her in that apartment, the rape wouldn't have happened. So, now, I didn't want her going back to that apartment, which she still maintained. (Her sister was living in it now.)

"Mary Lou, I swear; I'll do it this time. I'll quit for good. Please!" After several minutes of not succeeding in changing her mind, I slammed the phone down.

It wasn't just a "my girlfriend is leaving me, I'm going to kill myself" episode that I'm describing to you. My yearning for peace, for sleep, was the culmination of a lot of things--the constant, daily struggle that was slowly killing my spirit. I'm not looking for sympathy here. Shit, there are plenty of other people who have it way harder than I had it. But remember, knowing that doesn't make you feel any better. If I lost an arm, and somebody said, "Hey, I know a guy who lost two arms," am I going to feel any better? No, I don't think so. Compound this by the fact that the drugs made me feel hopeless--I knew I was not in control anymore--and you can see why this was indeed a really tough process that I was going through.

Dying seemed easier.

Looking down the subway tunnel for the final time, I saw lights still pretty far away--two small dots. I continued crying as I walked to the edge of the platform; my toes were now on the thick yellow line painted at the edge of the partially rotting wood. The decision was made.

I closed my eyes and dropped my head forward, as if diving sloppily into a pool with no grace or form. I did not want to see the track bed as I fell towards it, about five feet below. I'd like to think that I would have covered my face with my hands as I tumbled down, but I really don't remember. (Discovering later that I hadn't any serious injuries to my hands or arms—but only to my head--I can conclude that I must not have tried to protect my head at all.) I have no recollection of what happened next.

I'm told that several women screamed, and then a couple of guys jumped down to the tracks and managed to lift me off of them before the train got there, which may have taken another minute or so. Maybe, subconsciously, I was hoping it would go exactly like this. I mean, my Aunt Audrey jumped immediately before the train came in; she timed it perfectly to ensure her death. I jumped while the train was still approaching. Maybe, on some level, I wanted to be saved; maybe I hoped Mary Lou would come back, once she, and everyone else for that matter, finally knew just how desperate and unhappy I actually was.

I broke my neck, mangled my right knee and suffered several body and head cuts and contusions from the fall.

Now, not only was I despondent over the thought that Mary Lou was gone from my life forever, but I was permanently, physically changed; and I had put my family through yet another tragic event. To this day, I cannot raise my chin up high enough to shave properly; nor can I turn my head from side to side. Neck pain has become a constant companion. When I eventually got out of the hospital, I decided that this was the absolute last chance for me to get better; I vowed to kick drugs once and for all, and start my life over. Sadly enough, though, even then I could not do it.

Molested in An Ambulance?

At various times over the years I have tried in vain to recall my rescue from the subway tracks, and the subsequent ambulance ride to the hospital. In New York City, it seems that when you are knocked out after an accident--of course I use the term "accident" loosely here-- and you cannot provide proof that you have any medical insurance, then, you are usually whisked off to a city-run hospital.

I was taken to Woodhull Hospital--a sprawling, ominous-looking institution located in the Bedford Stuyvesant-section of Brooklyn. This was once a predominately Jewish, middle-class neighborhood; but by 1988, it had morphed into a very poor and rough area with burned-out buildings and high crime rates. I vaguely remember my mom and stepfather John in the hospital's Emergency Room, nervously trying to sort out what was happening with me. I remember noise, yelling, and utter chaos. My mother told me later that there were victims of stabbings and gunshots waiting for treatment, and that the ER floor was covered with blood. Any questions regarding my condition were answered rudely by surly, seemingly un-caring clerks and technicians.

Many hours after I was brought in, examined and x-rayed, I was abruptly released—even though I was bloodied, bruised and swollen, scraped and cut. I should never have been released. I couldn't walk right; with each step, it felt like I was almost going to fall down. (I found out later that my knee cartilage was completely torn to shreds.) My head was wobbling awkwardly on top of my neck; and my neck felt weak, with compromised stability. (It felt like my head was sitting atop one of those Slinky spring toys I had when I was six-years old.) I kept my palm against my chin to hold up my head as I was driven to my mom's apartment to recover.

Why wasn't I sent over to the G building at Kings County Psychiatric Center for a 90-day observation like most people who attempt suicide in NYC? I guess the doctors probably figured I'd just fallen from being intoxicated. It's pretty sad though, as I'm sure that you are supposed to at least be evaluated. I mean, think of how many others, released too quickly, may have gone right back out there and succeeded in ending their lives-- when they could have been helped by being held and treated for three months.

After lying in severe pain and trying to balance my head for the entire weekend, I realized that something was terribly wrong and that I needed to go back to the hospital. Since I was an Army veteran, my mom took me to the Brooklyn VA Hospital. The ER doctors sent me to the X-ray department after I explained to them how I had to hold my head up with my hand. Of course I lied about the details of how I'd "fallen" onto the subway tracks.

After being X-rayed, I was sitting in the waiting room, leaning the back of my head up against the wall when the X-ray tech, two doctors, and a nurse all came running up to the intake desk. When I heard the commotion, I looked over and saw them all sporting an urgent look in their eyes, carrying papers and large X-ray sheets that were flopping back and forth. They reminded me of the "Three Stooges" scenes I used to see as a kid on TV. You know, when they all run in together and stop short so quickly that their feet would actually go sliding along the floor until they finally came to a complete stop. I was wondering what the emergency was.

The desk clerks were busy on the phone while also trying to deal with impatient vets standing on line, but the obviously agitated medical team interrupted the clerks, asking excitedly, with raised voices: "Where is this guy, where is this guy?" One annoyed clerk looked at the paperwork, and pointed to the area where I was waiting. Sitting there, chin in hand, I recoiled in horror as the manic-looking group now quickly approached me. They yelled, "Are you Jerry Castaldo?"

"Yeah, whattsa matta?" I asked.

"Don't move, sit completely still or you could become paralyzed for life!" one of the doctors blurted out.

I thought to myself: *What the hell are they talking about? I've been moving around for three days now-- although with great difficulty.*

Since everyone else in the waiting room had heard all of this, high drama and tension ensued. I sat perfectly still while a long wooden board was brought in on a gurney. I was carefully lifted, and placed prone onto the board. I heard the sound of duct tape being torn off of a roll. The tape was then pressed firmly across my forehead and down each side of my head, past my ears and under the wooden board on which I was resting. Doctors explained to me that Woodhull Hospital had somehow missed seeing on the X-rays that my neck was broken; they never should have released me. I felt tears well up.

It's much easier to end your life—or want to end your life--while you are under the influence of alcohol or drugs. But by now I was completely sober. I was no longer fearless and ready to die. (Which is why I believe that 90-day observation-periods for attempted suicides can be life savers; people sober up, get better, and then realize that they'd be in a box in the ground had it not been for psychiatric intervention.) I was scared shitless.

I had only been in a helicopter once in my life, back when I was stationed in Germany. I remembered it being a dizzying, swaying ride. When I was told that I'd now be taken by helicopter to the better-equipped Manhattan VA Hospital, where neurosurgeons would operate, I was perplexed. *Isn't it better to be gently transported by ambulance?* I wondered. Why this dramatic flight to travel less than nine miles to Manhattan?

While lying there waiting to fly out above the Belt Parkway, past the Verrazano Bridge and Statue of Liberty, and into Manhattan, I was hit with a flurry of intense emotions. Especially after I had asked a doctor what was going to be done and got the dreaded news that I needed immediate surgery on my neck. After three hours of lying completely still, I was starting to get this aching pain in my lower back. I had experienced this pain on-and-off for my entire life; it usually only started when I was stationary during sleep for extended periods of time. In the past, as long as I could shift to another position, I could make the pain subside. Only recently-- many years after the events I'm describing occurred— have I been diagnosed with Spinal Stenosis, a painful, congenital narrowing of the spinal canal that has no cure and is progressive.

"Excuse me, doctor," I said. "I'm having bad pain. I need to move my legs over just a little bit, OK?" But the doctor told me not to move; if I moved, I was told again that I would risk paralysis. Over the next hours, as I started getting more and more pain, I kept asking the same question, always getting the same answer.

Now, twelve full hours had passed. No helicopter, no movement. You never realize how hard it is to stay completely still until you are actually forced to do it. I felt like I was being tortured. The doctors finally gave up waiting for the requested helicopter, and summoned a private ambulance to transport me.

Two uniformed ambulance drivers—a father, who was in his early sixties and a son who was about forty— helped ER personnel put me into the ambulance. I had been strapped down at my ankles, thighs, waist and chest, with my arms at my side. My head was secured on each side by what I can only describe as a giant vise. You can't really imagine what this feels like until you actually experience it. I was wrapped in a tightly woven cocoon and the only thing exposed was my face. My first thought was, *What if there's a fire?*

I felt helpless--powerless and vulnerable. It was scary, being immobilized like that. I mean, you couldn't scratch an itch if you wanted to; a bug could crawl into your nose and you couldn't stop it. You were really trapped.

Someone could even sexually assault you.

The whole situation seemed surreal to me. I felt imprisoned; I was in pain; I was distressed over the emotional and physical trauma that I'd gone through. And now, here I was in this old-fashioned "cracker box" type of ambulance. The driver--the older of the two men, the father--was isolated in the front cab. The younger man, his son--fat, sloppily dressed, in need of a haircut, and with an expression on his face that conjured up thoughts of "Duh"--was in the back with me.

The ride to the other hospital would take about a half hour, I estimated. It wasn't rush-hour; should be smooth sailing. Maybe they could give me something for the pain; I needed relief. I couldn't hold still for much longer. Panic was setting in.

After being on the highway for about 10 minutes, the guy in the back with me whispered that he had to check my vitals. There was only a dim light illuminating the area where I lay immobile. Shouldn't there be more light back here, I thought? He started opening my pants and lowered my front zipper. *"What the fuck is he doing? I guess it's OK, though; he's a professional medical person. What do I know?"*

He started pressing down on my abdomen and continued down to my pubic area. This went on for a while. I can't remember if it was fifteen seconds or thirty seconds, or two minutes or five minutes. After a while I blurted out: "Is everything OK?" He abruptly stopped, and closed up my pants. It took me months later to realize what he was doing. I just didn't see it at the time. How low and how depraved a person he was to take advantage of an injured patient being brought to the hospital. How many other helpless people had he "gone all the way" with? What a scumbag.

Giant Ice Tongs on My Head!

"Jerry, don't move. The doctor said you can't move," my mom uttered in a nervous, hushed tone usually reserved for conversations during burial ceremonies. She and my stepfather John hovered above me after my arrival at the Manhattan VA Hospital.

"I can't, Ma; I have to. I can't take it." With that I bent my knees and shifted my legs to the side. We all expected my spinal cord to snap at any moment. I didn't give a shit, it was that bad. I'd wait until the pain was unbearable, then I'd shift again. A nurse screamed at me. I yelled back.

"Hi, I'm Dr. Doyle," said the neurosurgeon who finally showed up two hours later, after having been paged at home. I guessed that he was in his late 30's. He was wearing a very worn and scuffed brown leather bomber-jacket, faded jeans, and boots. (I thought: *This is my doctor?*) He continued, "We have to stabilize your neck immediately, so I'm going to place you in traction. Try not to move while I get the equipment."

About a half hour passed before Dr. Doyle returned and announced that the only equipment available was over at NYU Medical Center, with which he was affiliated. He said he would be back from there as soon as possible.

And I'm trying my best to make sense of all this. I'm thinking: *"What? The doctor has to go pick the stuff up by himself? What is this?"*

Another hour passed before he returned. I couldn't believe my eyes. Dr. Doyle was walking over to me carrying what looked like giant steel ice-tongs, some pulley wheels, and a long section of chain. Between what he was wearing and what he was carrying, he could have easily been mistaken for a tow-truck driver getting ready to shackle up some stranded motorist's car.

"I'll tell you this--it won't be as bad as it looks," Dr. Doyle said. "The injections I have to give you in both temple areas will probably sting a bit more than what you'll feel while I'm applying this halo to your head." He then suggested that I hold on to my mom's hand and count to ten, as this would be a giant needle containing quite a bit of solution that had to be delivered very slowly. My eyes bugged out as I gazed upon this huge, cartoonish-looking needle. It reminded me of a slim baby bottle.

Did it hurt?

The anesthetic burned intensely as it went in. And then--after the temple areas of my head were sufficiently numb--the "halo" was placed down around my head. The idea of this contraption was to drive the two spikes into each side of my head, just above the ears. The points of each spike had to penetrate the scalp and delve only deep enough into the actual skull-bone to "grab" my head tightly. There were two giant thumbscrews on each side. While a nurse held the halo aloft, Dr. Doyle started turning the thumbscrews, all the while explaining that I would now feel pressure as this device closed around my head. What's weird is that while I could feel my head being squeezed together, I was only thinking how the squeaking of the long, bolt-like screws being turned sounded like they needed some oil. Was this thing rusty?

Halo on, pain medication finally administered, big weights hanging behind the bed via the pulley setup; I was content. For the next few weeks, I was a guest of the US Government. No phone, no amenities, and no ability to sit up--not even to see out the window.

During the next few days, the decision was made to implant two French-made, Roy Camille steel plates and four screws at the C-3 and C-4 vertebrae-area of my neck. For the next three months, walking would be difficult too, because the doctors had to wait for my spine to stabilize before they could operate on my knee.

This would be the second time that joining the US Army had saved my life.

Jerry Castaldo

Emergency Rooms, Jail and Bellevue

Winter-Spring 1989–Age 30

#1 song on the radio: "Like a Prayer"–Madonna

The huge International Beauty Show is presented every year at the Javits Convention Center in New York City. Tens of thousands of licensed beauty professionals converge on the site to see what's new in the industry.

In November--a month before I violently broke my neck falling to the subway tracks--I had landed a job as Master of Ceremonies for this glitzy event. I'd be working for three consecutive days in March. The pay would be excellent, and I'd get to sing at various times during each day-long, marathon-like show. But the Jerry Castaldo who reported for the first meeting in advance of the event was not quite the same man that they'd hired.

"Oh my God, Jerry--what happened?" asked a shocked Paul Davidson as he stared at the huge, beige foam-and-plastic cervical collar wrapped around my neck.

I replied cheerfully to him as I struggled into his car, "It's nothing. Don't worry! It'll be off by the time we do the show."

Paul Davidson was the executive who'd hired me years before to host the national tour for Revlon. And in November, he'd convinced his colleagues to hire me for the International Beauty Show. It was now a freezing day in mid-January, and here I was in Norwalk, Connecticut for a luncheon meeting with him and several other executives involved with the upcoming event. This would

184

be their first meeting with the man who'd be emceeing their show in March.

I must have been quite a disturbing sight for them to see--not only was I wearing that unsightly neck brace, I was moving stiffly and limping badly, with the aid of an aluminum cane.

That morning I'd taken an Amtrak train from Grand Central Terminal. Paul had come to pick me up at the train station in Norwalk. I'd tried to calm him by claiming that I'd simply been in a car accident—I couldn't tell him what had really happened in the subway—and I'd told him not to worry. I said I was sure that by the time of the Beauty Show in March I'd have the collar off and I'd be OK. And now—about an hour after arriving in Norwalk, sitting there in the restaurant with Paul and three of his colleagues--I could tell that the executives were nervous about me, despite my repeated reassurances.

I'd only been out of the hospital about a week before this meeting. My father had picked me up from the VA Hospital and then unceremoniously deposited me at my apartment. I wouldn't see him again for almost a full year. He had continued to drift in and out of my life ever since I was a teenager. I had noticed that whenever he was disappointed in me because I was in trouble, he'd be gone. This time was no different. But I have to say, I don't really blame him.

I got through the luncheon meeting, and returned to New York City. With nothing going on in my life from now until the March shows, I figured I'd just have to stay home and try to heal. My neck was causing me agonizing pain and I wasn't able to sit up in a chair for more than an hour or two at a time before I'd be forced to lie down again. The loneliness and depression wore on me. On top of that, I was absolutely broke. I needed to raise some cash.

Deciding I needed to buy some barbiturates to ease the pain and the sadness that I was feeling, I searched my apartment for things that I could sell. Focusing in on my beautiful, 27" Sony Trinitron television set, sitting on its custom-made stand, made me feel terribly guilty--but I gave in.

With a blinding snowstorm snarling mid-day traffic on East 14th Street in Manhattan, I was a sorry, pathetic sight. Adorned with my ever-present neck brace, and still limping because the knee operation that I needed from the subway fall wasn't scheduled until late March, I dragged the 120-pound TV through the deep snow on a small dolly. When I finally got to the pawn shop on Second Avenue, the gruff proprietor immediately recognized me. I'd been in many times before with guitars, speakers, and anything else I could get a loan on. He wrote the ticket and shoved $225.00 through the partition for this new TV—for which, I might add, I had paid over $1,200.00 less than a year before. I have little recollection of the following weeks as I was in a drug- and alcohol-induced blackout....

Maybe she felt bad about abandoning me during my hospital stay. Or maybe she felt sympathy for me from all of my pleading on the phone from the subway platform before I fell. Or maybe she just plain missed me and wanted to again try and help me. But—whatever the reason might have been--Mary Lou came back into my life just as the Javits Center shows were about to start. She and I had a long talk, and I made my usual promises to straighten out. For the next few days I got myself together. I reported to the convention center early for the first show, rarin' to go. I actually got through a couple of hours OK....

"Where's Jerry? You know, the MC--the guy with the tux on--have you seen him?" Paul Davidson was frantically asking the stagehands. We were now about three hours into the show and I had disappeared from the stage.

Hearing him toss about my name, I yelled to him, "Paul, Paul; I'm over here."

Paul rushed behind the huge curtain obscuring the backstage area from the audience and asked me, "What are you doing? Jerry, how come you're not out there?"

Not seeing any other way for me to find relief, I'd taken three metal folding-chairs and lined them up so that I could lie down across them. I'd put my neck collar on again, too. I explained to Paul that I had a lot of pain and needed to rest for a few minutes. He was not happy. Well, look at it from his point of view--here is this company paying me more than $1,000.00 per day and I'm lying down on the job!

To make matters worse, as the day wore on I started taking a Valium here and there; the Valium only made my performing skills disintegrate. Imagine me as a drugged up version of a beleaguered Jerry Lewis during the last hours of his own annual telethons for Muscular

Dystrophy. At the end of the third day, Paul had me follow him to a back office; he opened a safe, handed me several thousand dollars in cash, and coldly said goodbye.

Having that much money suddenly become available was extremely dangerous for me back then. On the way home, I stopped at a florist to pick up a huge, expensive flower arrangement for Mary Lou, detoured again to pick up some Chinese food for us, and then made a quick pit stop to my dealer. The days that followed were all a blur.

Then came a moment that hit me hard, a moment I'll never forget. I came home one day and discovered that Mary Lou had left for me on the dining-room table a long handwritten note. After reading it, I ran hurriedly to her bedroom closet. Sure enough, the closet was empty; only hangers remained. After so many years of arguments over my inability to stay sober, and many false exits, she was actually gone. I've never once seen her since then. And 21 years have now passed since that day. For me, the hardest part was not being able to talk or even say goodbye before she left--but if was for the best. She deserved more; she deserved peace.

From that March until late summer I would log no less than 13 visits to Emergency Rooms--convulsing, OD-ing, having to be stitched up and X-rayed. There were also arrests, overnights in roach-infested precinct lockups, and court appearances. I also reluctantly sublet my apartment and went back to Brooklyn to live with my mom as I kept missing paying the rent.

At one point I'd become so desperate that I asked my dealer for some pills and then--not caring that I didn't have the money to pay for them—I simply shoved them quickly into my mouth and swallowed them, right there on the spot. The dealer and his partner then started beating me to the ground. Once I was down, they just kept kicking me in the head and body until people on the street started yelling for someone to call the police. At that point, of course, the dealer and his partner ran away. I remember a crowd assembling around me to help as I slowly got up. I waved them off, thanking them as I smiled and quietly thought to myself: *That wasn't too bad...* A few days before had been much worse, because then I'd almost lost consciousness after being choked up against a wall by this giant bear of a guy in a dark, filthy crack house down in Alphabet City.

This fun-filled year also marked one other milestone for me: I made it to the big-time of all psychiatric hospitals, Bellevue. As a kid, I used to love to watch the movie *Miracle on 34th Street,* which would always air around Christmas-time. I remember the jolly character Kris Kringle being admitted to Bellevue because they deemed him crazy for insisting that he was the one and only Santa Claus. Now, here I was, in America's oldest public hospital, once again trying to convince a psychiatrist that I "wasn't crazy." Although I do remember thinking at the time: *Wait, could it be that maybe I really am crazy?*

Eastern Airlines Honors Me

"Hi! My name is Jerry Castaldo and I've got to speak quickly here and make you understand that I can help you. That's right! I can help you by making your job easier. Just look into my eyes; can you see it? You do, right? You can see that I'm highly motivated and that I'll be a hard worker for Eastern Airlines. Don't pass on me and you'll have someone you'll be glad you hired," I said as if I were a seasoned carnival barker.

I'd seen an ad in the newspaper; Eastern Airlines was looking for flight attendants. The ad described a month-long training-period in Miami with all expenses paid, plus a salary. Since I didn't have my apartment and there was absolutely nothing else happening--no shows, no regular job, no girlfriend --, this sounded perfect. This would be another chance for a new start. Never mind the fact that I was in the throes of addiction, worse than ever before.

The pleasant, well-dressed black man who was interviewing potential flight attendants initially seemed a bit taken aback by my aggressive pitch. But I could see his reaction gradually shift to intrigue. He smiled, and I noticed him putting my paperwork on top of a very short stack of papers instead of depositing it into the big plastic bin next to his chair. Relief set in! I'd waited for hours on an incredibly, long, snaking line. He handed me a ticket with a number on it, pointed, and said, "OK, go over to that area and you'll be interviewed again by the people there as soon as they can get to you."

There were over one thousand men and women clogging the terminal here at La Guardia airport with hopes of getting these jobs. I knew that I'd just be another face in the crowd if I didn't do something to stand out. My "look me in the eyes" routine had gotten me out of the psych ward in Germany many years before, and now it had proved successful again on this day. After four more consecutive interviews by separate screeners, which lasted late into the evening, I was hired.

In less than a month I was in glorious Miami Beach, staying at an expensive and very beautiful high-rise hotel that boasted spectacular views of the Atlantic Ocean. I had a male roommate, and each morning we'd board a chartered bus to the Miami Airport for our daily training and classes. Since ninety percent of my classmates were young women who looked like fashion models, it was really kind of fun being one of only a few males.

In the third week of training, my roommate told me that some of the other students were asking him what the deal was with his roommate. This was because I never socialized outside of school or the airport cafeteria. Every night I stayed in my room studying manuals; I'd never go out with the others to the clubs or bars. Instead, on weekdays each morning I would rise at 4:30 am, swim laps in the pool, then run the beach for miles, shower, and be ready for the bus by 7 am. The weekends were no different; I stayed close to the hotel.

The difficulty level of the intense emergency training we were being given was surprising to me. We had to memorize schematics of several types of planes, and learn how to remove and get out of windows, doors, and tail cones--often in simulated smoky and chaotic conditions. Many people think of flight attendants as "waiters and waitresses," but the food-and-drink-serving primer was given only on the last two days; everything else we were taught involved saving peoples' lives.

There were about 60 of us in all, seeking to become flight attendants; and each week several trainees were cut and sent home--some crying. It reminded me of being in the Army during basic training, when people were shipped out after failing to keep up.

~

"Ladies and gentlemen, Eastern Airlines is now proud to announce our 'Model Flight Attendant' for this training cycle. Please put your hands together for Mr. Jerry Castaldo," the Vice President for Southeast Operations announced from the stage.

During the last week of training, we were all instructed to vote for whomever we felt should be awarded the title of "Model Flight Attendant." And now I was receiving this top honor; I'd garnered the most votes from my fellow trainees. And frankly, I was stunned.

I made my way down the aisle and up to the stage as the music played. My fellow classmates (plus any of their family members who'd flown in for the graduation ceremony) were applauding wildly. I was given a plaque that held my diploma and a shiny gold keychain with the Eastern Airlines logo on it.

Several of the girls with whom I'd trained were going to be sharing an apartment in Manhattan after graduation. One of them who I'd become friendly with, gave me the address and phone number. Even though I'd gotten myself back into good shape physically--and had gotten myself sober--I just couldn't maintain it. Within two months, I was at that girl's apartment drinking heavily again-- and at one point running barefoot like a madman out into the dirty Chelsea streets to score coke. That same night I was scheduled to fly to Port Au Prince, Haiti, for a four-day trip up and down the eastern seaboard. When I reported for work at La Guardia Airport, I was deemed unfit for duty and sent home.

The next day, after I'd sobered up, depression set in because I realized that I had fucked up yet again. I was just unable to hold things together. I was sure that I was fired. And I was so embarrassed that I didn't even bother to show up for the flights on my schedule during the next few days. The VP who had originally hired me left several voice messages saying that he really liked me and that I should come in to talk; that he'd give me another chance.

Eastern Airlines wanted their "Model Flight Attendant" back.

Banished from Mexico's Club Med

"Ah-oooh! Ah-oooh!" I howled at the bright silver moon as I drove along the shoreline, the right side of the pickup-truck's tires parting the incoming waves that were crashing ashore. "Ah-oooh!"

Following my awkward departure from Eastern Airlines, I'd quickly called a booker at Club Med who months before had offered me a gig. He said that I could be part of a troupe that would entertain guests at one of their West Coast Mexican resorts. A plane ticket was Fed-Exed to my mom's apartment; I grabbed my guitar and suitcase, and headed for tropical Playa Blanca.

Now, here in Mexico, full of Puerto Rican rum consumed on an empty stomach, I'd been transformed into a werewolf! A drunken werewolf! A drunken werewolf driving a stolen truck! Well, technically, I guess it wasn't really stolen; I'd just borrowed it and planned to return it later. On the way back to my cabana I'd stumbled upon this shabby Ford truck parked outside of the resort's kitchen, keys dangling invitingly in the ignition. I missed driving so.

During the next few months, wearing little more than a tiny little male bikini or sometimes a brightly colored sarong, I'd gone on a total blitz of drink, food, promiscuous sex, and general depravity. On more than one occasion I'd almost drowned in the unforgiving, rough waters between our resort and a small offshore island, attempting what we called the "Margarita Kayak Run." The Activities Calendar, listing things to do each day, would announce that at 4 pm you could take a kayak and paddle way out to this island; once you got there, you would chug unlimited free Margaritas before paddling back through the churning Pacific Ocean. What a stupid idea!

This hedonistic existence came to a screeching halt one bright morning. I came shuffling in, very slowly, to the resort's huge outdoor dining area at breakfast-time-- my neck limp and head hung forward, my eyes squinting in the sunlight as I struggled to find my table. I was wearing only my wet underpants, and they sported a disturbing mosaic of dark stains on the backside; I was dragging my soaking-wet jeans lazily along the floor behind me. All the guests here were assigned to specific tables for all meals during their stay, so I kept struggling to raise my head up to see where my table was. After finally seeing the conservative-looking group of people that I recognized from our past meals together, I navigated toward them for breakfast. By now dozens of stunned guests and wide-eyed servers had all started pointing and murmuring. No one knew what to do.

"I'm zorry, I'm zorry," I mumbled to my horrified table-mates as I very carefully slid into my chair to sit down with them. "I'm zo zorry; really I am. I'm zorry," I whimpered to them, pleading for forgiveness. "I juzt have ta eat sumpin', pleaze, I gotta eat. Zorry."

Behind me I'd left a long, winding, narrow puddle of brown water, courtesy of my trailing jeans. Earlier, just as the sun was coming up, I'd been so drunk and feeling ill, that I thought I should go to the pool and submerge my head into the water and maybe I'd feel better. Instead, the smell of the chlorine made me start vomiting right into the pool, which then triggered a deadly attack of uncontrollable diarrhea. I can remember the stupefied look on the face of the older Mexican man who was skimming the pool down at the far end. He watched with great curiosity as I proceeded to remove my jeans in slow motion, and then try to clean them off by dunking them in and out of the water.

Since this was not my first egregious offense at the resort, I was given some pesos, placed in a taxi, and driven 90 miles to the airport where a flight would take me out of Mexico. The people running the resort just wanted me out--immediately.

Wandering aimlessly and drunk around the run-down section of Puerto Vallarta while waiting to fly back to New York, I remember that I was almost mugged--no doubt because the locals could see the condition I was in. I remember, too, going into a dirty storefront restaurant that had live chickens in crates, right out in plain sight. The place was gross, but I was so hungry, and every other place seemed to be closed at this late hour. The counter guy told me in broken English to go sit at the table near the window and he'd bring me my chicken dinner when it was ready. I figured that this was OK so long as when he put the plate down in front of me, there was nothing on it that was still moving.

The next day, sitting on the runway waiting for the plane to take off, I started to feel sick. And all I could think was: *I must have eaten an infected chicken....*

The Friars Club Debacle

Spring 1990–Age 31

#1 song on the radio: "Vogue"--Madonna

After arriving back in New York, I felt emotionally bankrupt. Just one year before I had been telling people excitedly, with that real gift for rationalizing things that I had: "Oh, it's good that that happened to me down in the subway--because it was what I really needed to jolt me into cleaning up, once and for all. Now I'll be able to find the strength I need to change...."

How very naïve I was.

The depressing reality was: I was now starting to believe I might be doomed to ride the same old merry-go-round forever. I was experiencing a general sense of malaise. I felt numb, discouraged; I had lost all confidence. This routine had to stop. It had been going on for years and years: *screw up, straighten out, do well for a while, relapse, repeat....*

Shaking off all of those negative feelings, I took a deep breath, and soon found employment at the exclusive Excelsior Health Club in Manhattan. This was no time for me to think about singing. I figured I could get back to that later. Right now, I needed money to stabilize my situation. So I decided that I was going to work--around the clock, if I had to. After a few months at the Excelsior Club, I no longer needed to sublet my apartment and I was happy to have it back. I decided that I could also fill any free hours I had with another job: *Since I've lost*

*just about everyone in my life, what do I care about
having any free time for myself?*

My mind raced as I furiously scoured the *New York
Times* "Help Wanted" section. Seeing the words "Show
Business Club" stopped me dead in my tracks. Spying a
tiny box ad that did not give an address or a phone
number, but only a Post Office Box number, I read:
"Prestigious Show Business Club in Midtown needs
Director of Fitness for its Health Club." I started thinking;
thinking, thinking... *I know it! The Friars Club--that has to
be it!*

Growing up I'd seen the *Dean Martin Celebrity Roasts*
on television and was always intrigued by the mystery of
"the business." I'd read somewhere that the Friars Club
has been wining and dining the top personalities of the
times since 1904. Show business in general has been
fascinating to me since I was a kid. I wondered so many
things: *What are those people like? How do they get to
where they are? How do I get in? Can I get in? Who do
you have to know? Is talent always necessary? It doesn't
always appear to be a prerequisite for fame.....*

On Monday morning at 7:30, I was dressed in a
traditional navy-blue business suit, armed with a
briefcase, and standing vigil outside the front door of the
famous Friars Club on 55th Street between Park Avenue
and Madison Ave. Of course, I knew that I could be
wrong, there was always a chance that the ad was not
for this place--but I couldn't risk not trying. If this *was* the
right place, I could imagine an avalanche of mail would
soon be falling onto the person screening applicants; I
didn't want my letter and resume getting lost in the

shuffle. If I was correct, I was now going to beat everyone to the punch.

"Hi, excuse me; do you know who does the hiring of the staff here?" I posed this question to the first person I saw headed to the front door. He happened to be a cook who gave me the names of Michael Caputo and Jean-Pierre Trebot. These were the two men that I would need to see. So for the next hour and a half, I questioned anyone who looked French or anyone who could pass for a New York Italian. Then—bingo!--Michael Caputo replied, "Yes, I am. Who are you?"

I explained to Michael that I suspected he was looking for a director for the health club upstairs, and I was hoping that if I was correct, he'd be impressed by my deciphering the cryptic ad I'd seen. He confirmed that yes, he had indeed placed the ad and that yes, he hadn't put more info in it because he didn't want a stampede of people coming to the club in person.

After urging him to interview me formally, I was brought in to his office. In the next week, I got two people for whom I'd worked in health clubs to write glowing letters of recommendation for me. Subsequently, after two more interviews, I was told that I had the job. When I showed up for my first day, Michael said there were hundreds of applicants vying for the job, but that my sheer enthusiasm had won them over. I was in!

Sober and focused again--albeit "white knuckling" it as in the past--I really felt that this might be it for me. If I could just walk the straight and narrow, I could relinquish this "regular job" and get back to doing shows. Nothing would stop me now. This club was going to be the beginning of everything for me; where my ability, drive, and hard work would meet the needed connections--the power brokers. I just knew it and felt it. This wasn't a guess; I was absolutely sure of it.

Right before I'd gotten this job, I'd met and had begun dating a recent Cornell graduate, Leigh, who was ten years my junior and just starting out on Wall Street. Her apartment was not far from the Friars Club, and each night when I'd finish, I could walk right down the block to meet with her. At this time I'd also met a brilliant young lawyer, Ira, who had recently graduated from Harvard. We'd met at another health club and since I'd shared some of my sordid past with him, he was happy for me to be moving in the right direction. It was a high point for me to have both Leigh and Ira surprise me by taking me to dinner to celebrate my getting the job. Compared to the way things had been going for me just six months before, my life now felt pretty close to spectacular!

This whirlwind of upward mobility both socially and at the club continued. One member who had a private plane would invite me to fly regularly. I enjoyed conversations about growing up with stars like Norman Fell and Jack Warden. It was great. One day I'd be joking with songwriter Sammy Cahn, then the next day it would be former Mayor Abe Beame. If I wasn't trying to cajole comedian Richard Belzer into the gym to work out, I was hanging out with Broadway and film star Len Cariou while he was walking on the treadmill. One night a top agent from the William Morris Agency asked me to jump into his Cadillac and accompany him to a show to "cover" one of his clients; a major country star.

I thought to myself: *Thank God for this job. It will only be a matter of time before I can reveal to all of my new acquaintances that I'm really a performer at heart, that performing is what I'm truly meant to do for a career. For now, though, I've got to bide my time for a bit and accept that I'm still just the club's Director of Fitness.*

Looking back, it's very easy for me to pinpoint the exact moment when all of this good fortune came crashing down. There was a precise moment when I needed to make a choice, the correct choice. As all addicts do, though--without an external support system to help them weather precarious situations such as the one I was about to encounter--I ultimately became my own saboteur.

"A toast everyone--you too, Jerry, someone give Jerry a glass," renowned comedian Alan King ordered. He had been regaling us with anecdotes and had a semi-circle of people, a venerable who's who of show business, around him.

Because many of the members had taken a liking to me, I was starting to be invited onto the other floors of the building, as well as into the dining room to eat. Because I was staff—an employee, not a member of the club--I'd been instructed to stay in the top-floor gym. So it really should not have come as a surprise to me that Michael and Jean-Pierre called me into their office one day to remind me of this policy. I then challenged them by pointing out that during these forays of mine into members-only areas, I was off-duty and out of uniform. They looked at each other, shrugged, and said they'd talk about it and get back to me. I felt that although they wanted their members to feel that there was an exclusivity to the club, they didn't want to offend any members, either, if those members were treating me as their guest.

I continued accepting invitations from the members when I was off-duty, and my superiors--while never officially condoning this--looked the other way and never mentioned it to me again. It was very exciting for me when one member who I'd shared my performing background with, spoke of possibly sponsoring me someday so that I, too, could become a member of the club—an actual Friar! This of course would mean that I couldn't work there anymore; instead, I'd be a member. And in truth, that was exactly the eventual outcome I had hoped for when I'd first seen the ad in the *Times*....

So I appreciated Alan King inviting me to toast now. As the bartender--who was technically my co-worker--ran toward me with a tray of martinis, I reached for the glass. This reminded me of being on the yacht in Florida with French playboy Philippe Junot some years before. I should have known better. In truth, I *did* know better. But still, I chose to drink from that glass.

Perhaps you've heard the old saying: *It starts with just one drink--the first drink.* Within a few short months after that congenial toast, I drank progressively more and more, and then reignited my relationship with drugs. Inevitably, I managed to alienate just about all of the new friends that I'd made at the club. Between my reporting for work in an obviously altered state or not reporting at all, members were whispering to each other: "What's wrong with Jerry?" And my late-night phone calls to members' homes didn't help either. The end was near.

One esteemed club member named Bob Mounty, with whom I'd become very friendly, led the charge against me. He was a powerful radio executive who hailed from Philadelphia and who was responsible for driving shock-jock Howard Stern out from WNBC. With the juice he provided, I was fired from the Friars Club and Michael Caputo escorted me out of the building. I reached out to the only friends that I had left, my new girlfriend Leigh and my friend Ira. But since both of them had also been witnessing my ugly transformation, neither one of them would return my phone calls. I never spoke to or saw either one of them again.

Being cast out from the Friars Club and being abandoned by everyone felt especially painful.

It would prove to be, however, the straw that would break the proverbial camel's back.

Recovery?

November 1st, 1990--Age 31

#1 Song on Radio: "Ice Ice Baby"--Vanilla Ice

The hopeless drudgery of my repeated quests for sobriety—trying to do it my own way--was now more than I could exist with. It was over. I knew I could not, and would not, ever be able to live a normal life, unless, unless I made some changes.

But I was still confused. I'd still rationalize. I'd tell myself: *To be an extraordinarily successful artist in any creative field, it's best if you suffer an inordinate amount of emotional pain and mental anguish. That would then magically deliver to you expertise not attainable by ordinary people....*

This was the distorted message I'd gotten from reading the life stories of so many greats in entertainment. And I bought into this fallacy. I told myself: *Oh good, this is actually to my advantage as an artist that I'm so fucked up....*

You really can make yourself believe anything.

For years, all of the well-meaning people in my life had relentlessly badgered me about how addiction is a recognized medical disease; they said it's not something that can be controlled by sheer willpower, and urged me to get help. Although I'd always thought such talk was bullshit, it finally got me thinking. Feeling a more acute fear and desperation gripping me this time, I thought back to a doctor who had treated me with charcoal during an ER visit after I'd overdosed. I remembered how he'd described to me "a really wonderful place" in which to get help, that happened to be right down the street from my apartment, off of Second Avenue. He'd written the name and address down on a piece of paper and urged me to go. The look in his eyes as he handed me the paper spoke volumes. It told me that he was serious and that he really cared. For a fleeting moment, I had felt comforted.

On October 31st, the annual Greenwich Village Halloween Parade was under way as I staggered drunkenly around the sidelines. I was just trying to distract myself and not think of how truly alone I now was. Obnoxious and talking loudly to just about everyone who entered into my fuzzy line of sight, I plodded along with no direction, lost.

Later that night, after I got back to my apartment, I pulled the suicide-hotline number from my desk drawer where I'd stashed it months before. I was making this call not because I felt like killing myself at that particular moment, but rather because I was desperate to talk to someone—anyone--to break the late-night loneliness I was feeling. I dialed with one eye closed, in order to focus in on the keypad, and started a maudlin conversation with the guy who answered. But he sounded cold, and at one point I even felt as if he was annoyed with me. It was like a bad "Saturday Night Live" skit; he had an "I don't really care much" kind of attitude. *What? People—perhaps hanging by just a thread--are calling this number, and they're gonna be counseled by him?!?* I hung up. And then a part of me wondered if I was just being paranoid.

Rummaging through the desk drawer again, I found the name of the place that the ER doctor had told me about, and stared for a while at the writing scribbled on the wrinkled piece of paper. I dragged myself into my bedroom, clutching the triangular scrap in my hand, and slept through the night.

Early the next morning, zombie-like, I climbed the dirty, worn steps up the narrow spiral stairwell to the fifth floor of "The 14th Street Workshop." I had decided that I would sit way in the back and not talk to anyone; I was still subconsciously rebelling. Sloppy handwritten signs, crookedly taped to the walls outside the tiny rooms, listed the different meetings and times: NA, AA, and OA. Choosing the AA room, I entered and plopped myself down with a thud onto an uncomfortable, paint-chipped folding-chair. Crossing my arms, I stared blankly ahead as I waited for the meeting to begin, the smell of brewing coffee and cigarettes permeating the air. As several smiling, happy-looking people started to trickle in, many embracing each other with oversized hugs, I thought to myself, "friggin' cult," and wanted to leave. I didn't move.

When the meeting finally ended--and before I could slip out of there unnoticed--a slight, friendly looking man stopped me and quickly introduced himself. His obviously sincere and heartfelt appeal made an enormous impact on me; he extended his hand to shake mine and said, "Come back again tomorrow, please. I promise you, it gets better."

The following day, I returned as he implored. The day after that I returned again; the next day again.

I sat attentively in those rooms, every single day--sometimes twice in a day--for the next full year and a half.

Jerry Castaldo

Epilogue

Summer 2010–Age 51

#1 song on the radio: None, anymore. Several different music charts by genre now.

I haven't a clue as to why it was on that one particular day, November 1st, 1990--after 14 grueling, long years of futile attempts to abstain from drugs and alcohol--that I would miraculously succumb to a complete and total surrender. I'm told that it just takes a longer time for some people, especially when addiction has got such a stranglehold on them. Those cramped meeting rooms-- and the benevolent people in them from whom I drew unconditional support and encouragement--became my absolutely last bastion, ultimately saving me.

Even as I celebrate nearly 20 years of sobriety, I'm not under the illusion that I am now safe, or that I'm fixed, or that all of this could never happen again. For that would be quite perilous.

It's widely understood in the field of treatment for substance-abuse that a lot of the core issues of addiction involve trauma. It's also believed that secrets keep people sick--and that is just one of many reasons why I accepted the formidable challenge of writing this book. Overall, it has been quite difficult for me as I've looked back, struggling to conjure up images and events that occurred during my active years so that I could chronicle them here. By doing so, I'm reminded of how often I'd failed.

Currently, my relationships with my parents, brother, extended relatives, and many old friends and business colleagues are intact and thriving; I consider those good relationships a tremendous reward for my staying clean. My father has been accompanying me on the road to about 200 of my 300 shows per year for the last sixteen years running, always beaming as he accepts accolades from enthusiastic audience members after my performances. My mother and stepfather are both retired now and they own a beautiful home in New York. My brother Ken is a National Registry Paramedic and Registered Nurse who has traveled the world with the US Air Force and Air National Guard. His crowning glory is his beautiful eleven-year-old daughter, Ashley.

Likewise, while I haven't attained real "celebrity" status, my performing career has flourished, giving me the financial freedom to maintain a comfortable home in a rural countryside setting. Since 1991, I've made my living solely by performing, and that's extremely satisfying to me. I'm doing exactly what I envisioned when I was just a seven-year-old first-grader, and I'm very grateful for the success that I've had. I'm also glad to report--since I was so passionate about driving as a teenager--that... oh, do I get to drive now! From small towns to big towns, traveling is my life, and I do love it.

Of course, we do not all live in a fairy tale. Rather than classify my long-term recovery as a "happy ending," I'd like to just call it what it really is--an ongoing process, a "happy beginning." I've still got plenty to do, much to learn, and even more to accomplish. There have been bumps in the road, such as the devastating emotions that rocked me after my mother and my cousin Ron

210

barely managed to escape lower Manhattan during the tragic events of September 11th, 2001. My poor mom should not have had to see in her lifetime what she witnessed on that terrible day. I faltered momentarily, but I did not fall. For now I possess the tools.

Finally, as unfortunate as it was for me and for those around me to have endured so many chaotic years while I tried in vain to overcome my affliction, my urgent message to those of you still out there who may feel trapped is simply this:

Take advantage of the great strides made in recent decades in the understanding of addiction by seeking out—right now--the help that's available. Please, do not waste half of your life--as I did--destroying opportunities and relationships. I learned, the hard way, that although I was filled to the brim with confidence and felt that I possessed an iron will, I just could not beat this thing on my own. If you suffer from addiction of any kind, I sincerely hope you aren't lulled into thinking that you may be different.

If just one person can say, "Wow, look at how messed up and hopeless he was, but look at him now at 20-years-clean," and take inspiration from that, then I'll feel that this book is worth something, that it's more than just a sad, depressing recounting of my life. Yes. I'd feel that I'd succeeded on a truly fantastic level--to actually have helped someone....

Thank you for reading my story.

Jerry Castaldo

About the Author

New York City born-and-bred. Jerry Castaldo is a well-reviewed musical entertainer, who consistently logs an average of 300 shows per year. He has opened for such stars as Jerry Seinfeld, David Brenner and Dom Deluise.

After singing and playing lead guitar in different bands during his early 20's, Castaldo put together a solo stage act and started singing standards from the Great American Songbook at nightspots in and around Manhattan. He gained further exposure via Joe Franklin's long-running television talk show.

Gaining recognition for his deft comedic skills and impressive "quick-on-his-feet" abilities, not just his singing, led him to landing countless master-of-ceremonies positions, such as hosting the International Beauty Show at the Javits Center in New York City and a 25-city national tour for Revlon Inc. industrial shows.

Castaldo has enjoyed playing such well-known venues as the Trump Plaza Hotel and Casino in Atlantic City, NJ, and the Waldorf Astoria Hotel (including benefits honoring Christopher Reeve and Ray Charles). His repertoire spans the eras—everything from big-band favorites (he has also performed in concert with the Sammy Kaye Orchestra) to contemporary standards.

The New York Times (C. Gerald Fraser) has noted of Castaldo: "He brings talent, enthusiasm, and energy to his work." The New York Post's Curt Davis has called him: "One of the best all-around entertainers in New York City."

July 2010 kicked off the Summer-Fall Celebrity Concert Series at the beautiful Center for Performing Arts Complex in Raleigh, NC. Castaldo was tapped to host and open the shows and do all regional radio spots for these events.

The million-selling record artists on the bill included Gary Lewis & the Playboys *("This Diamond Ring")*, Jay Black, formerly of Jay and the Americans *("This Magic Moment")*, Maureen McGovern *("The Morning After")*, Lou Christie *("Lightning's Striking")*, Marilyn McCoo & Billy Davis *("You Don't Have to be a Star")*, Maxine Nightingale *("Right Back to Where We Started From")*, tenor Michael Amante & B'way songstress Melba Moore.

Finally, Castaldo plans on recording a new CD which will include some of his original music. Obie-winning and Tony-nominated Broadway composer *Gary William Friedman* has contributed two songs to this project.

When not on the road performing, Castaldo enjoys living in the rolling hills of Hunterdon County in scenic western New Jersey with Buster, his black Lab and loyal running partner.

~

"I'm always interested in hearing from readers. Please feel free to email me or 'Friend' me on Facebook. I will always do my best to reply. You can also follow me on Twitter. Thanks!"   Jerry

www.jerrycastaldo.com

www.facebook.com/JerryCastaldo99

www.twitter.com/#!/JerryCastaldo

Jerry Castaldo

About the Editor

Chip Deffaa has written eight books, including *Swing Legacy, Voices of the Jazz Age, In the Mainstream, Traditionalists and Revivalists in Jazz, Jazz Veterans, F. Scott Fitzgerald: The Princeton Years* (ed.), *Blue Rhythms,* and *C'Mon Get Happy* (with David Cassidy). He has also contributed chapters to the books *Harlem Speaks* and *Roaring at One Hundred.*

He has written and directed in New York such plays as *George M. Cohan: In his Own Words* (published by Samuel French Inc.), *Yankee Doodle Boy* (Drama Source), *The George M. Cohan Revue* (Baker's Plays), *George M. Cohan & Co.,* Eldridge Plays), *The Seven Little Foys, The Johnny Mercer Jamboree,* and *Theater Boys.* He currently has a play that he's written and directed running Off-Broadway: *One Night with Fanny Brice.* The Associated Press says: "Deffaa has distilled Brice's busy life and career into a well-paced two-hour show." Joe Franklin (Bloomberg Radio) hails the show as "fresh and impressive... a true Golden-Age-of-Show-Business love story."

For 18 years, Deffaa wrote for *The New York Post.* He was also a longtime writer for *Entertainment Weekly* magazine.

Deffaa has written liner notes for many CD's, including those of such artists as Miles Davis, Benny Goodman, Ray Brown, Diane Schuur, Ruth Brown, Tito Puente, Dick Hyman, Randy Sandke, Scott Hamilton, and the Count Basie Orchestra. Deffaa has won an ASCAP/Deems Taylor Award, a New Jersey Press

Association Award, and an IRNE Award (Independent Reviewers of New England). Deffaa is a member of the Society of Stage Directors & Choreographers, the Dramatists Guild, ASCAP, NARAS, the Jazz Journalists Association, the F. Scott Fitzgerald Society, the Drama Desk, and the American Theatre Critics Association. Deffaa is a trustee of the Princeton *Tiger* magazine.

George M. Cohan Tonight!, which Deffaa wrote and directed Off-Broadway in New York at the Irish Repertory Theatre, was hailed by The New York Times as "brash, cocky, and endlessly euphoric" (The New York Times, March 11, 2006). It has been performed internationally, playing most recently at the New Players Theater on the West End in London. Deffaa's latest plays include *The Family that Sings Together...* (published by Drama Source), *Song-and-Dance Kids,* and *Fanny Brice & Co.* All of Deffaa's plays are available for licensing. He is represented by the Fifi Oscard Agency, New York City.